PUFFIN BOOKS

EVERY BODY

MOLLY FORBES

EVERY BODY

Illustrated by
MOLLIE CRONIN

PUFFIN BOOKS

PUFFIN BOOKS

UK | USA | Canada | Ireland | Australia
India | New Zealand | South Africa

Puffin Books is part of the Penguin Random House group of companies
whose addresses can be found at global.penguinrandomhouse.com.

www.penguin.co.uk   www.puffin.co.uk   www.ladybird.co.uk

First published 2024
001

Printed in China

The authorized representative in the EEA is Penguin Random House Ireland,
Morrison Chambers, 32 Nassau Street, Dublin D02 YH68

A CIP catalogue record for this book is available from the British Library

ISBN: 978–0–241–63936–8

All correspondence to:
Puffin Books, Penguin Random House Children's
One Embassy Gardens, 8 Viaduct Gardens
London SW11 7BW

For my daughters, Freya and Effie –
it's a privilege to be your mum.
M.F.

To my cousins, with love.
M.C.

Hello lovely reader. Thank you for being here.

This is just a short note to let you know that some of the things we explore in this book might feel tricky for you, so we have included a resources section at the back of the book for more information and support.

There is discussion of some big topics, including mental health, bullying, anti-fat bias and weight stigma, ableism, racism, colourism and gender discrimination. The text also briefly touches on eating disorders and disordered eating. If you are affected by any of these issues or if you feel worried or anxious about anything discussed in this book, it's always best to speak with a trusted adult and not try to manage these feelings on your own.

MF ♥

CONTENTS

WELCOME TO

EVERY BODY

(WHERE EVERYBODY
IS WELCOME)

There are more than eight billion bodies on this planet, but only one belongs to you. Every moment of every day, your body is hard at work breathing, moving and keeping you alive. To be honest, you probably don't give it enough credit. It's easy to forget how amazing your body is when you're busy doing other things. Like when you were checking your outfit in the mirror, you probably didn't notice your eyes blinking twenty times. Or when you stroked that new cosy jumper, you may not have been aware of the 3,000 touch receptors lighting up at the end of each of your fingers.

Your body is pretty incredible, but you might take it for granted. You might forget all the wonderful ways it lets you experience the world and instead worry about how it looks. I'll let you in on a secret: everyone feels bad about their body sometimes. Even celebrities with millions of followers on YouTube. Even your gran. Even your teacher. (Who knew teachers had feelings?)

BUT WHO AM I TO BE TELLING YOU THIS?

Hi, I'm Molly. I grew up way back in the 1990s, before the 90s were retro and before TikTok was even a thing. Back then, most of the people on the front of magazines were white, thin and non-disabled, which was what my body looked like too. And, even though my body kind of fitted the picture of what we were told 'good' bodies looked like, I still regularly felt bad about it – like it wasn't quite good enough. (By the way, the whole idea of 'good' bodies and 'bad' bodies belongs in the bin, but we'll get more into that later.) Remember, this was ages ago, so I didn't know what I know now. Today, I work with schools and organizations to help them understand what it means to embrace and respect all bodies. I even wrote a book about it for parents and teachers called *Body Happy Kids*. Oh, and I post funny pictures and videos of myself on Instagram, often pulling my best kitchen-disco mum moves, which makes my daughters cringe. (Sorry, kids.)

My hope is that, with this book, you will learn how to appreciate and respect both your own body and the bodies of those around you, even if they all look and function differently from one another. I also hope you'll be able to educate your friends and family on what good body image means.

This book is for everybody – and I mean that quite literally. Your hamster can even read it, if they can read (in which case, quick, get them on YouTube, because that is impressive). Everyone with a body is welcome here.

Along the way, you'll learn some new words to help how you think about bodies. These words will be in bold the first time they appear, and you can look them up in the glossary at the back of the book too. You will also hear from people with different body types who have stood up to prejudice and made the world a more accepting place for *everybody*. By the time you've finished reading, maybe you'll be ready to join them in their mission? With your help, we can let people know that all bodies are to be celebrated – including your own.

WELCOME TO EVERY BODY. I'M GLAD YOU'RE HERE.

CHAPTER 1
MY BODY

If you are a human, you have a body. And if you have a body, you will likely have thoughts and feelings about that body. This is called

BODY IMAGE.

Simple, right? Except it isn't.

The way we think and feel about our body is often far from simple. Our body changes constantly, and our feelings about it change too. The way our body is treated by other people can also affect how we feel about it.

Maybe you haven't thought much about body image before – in which case, GO YOU, because even most grown-ups think about it way too much. But perhaps you've noticed changes in your body that have made you feel a bit . . . weird. Or maybe you've heard people at school commenting on how other kids look and it's made you uncomfortable. Understanding body image can help you to work out why this stuff happens and what you can do about it.

You might be thinking, *I actually look fabulous all the time, so this doesn't apply to me.* Again, GO YOU and your fabulous style! But I have some news for you:

THERE'S MORE TO HAVING GOOD BODY IMAGE THAN BEING HAPPY WITH YOUR APPEARANCE.

Are you getting confused yet? Because I was very confused when I learned this.

BODY MYTH ALERT:

Positive body image is simply about liking what you see in the mirror.

Wrong! Positive body image is about *way* more than thinking you look good. In fact, getting too hung up on the way you look can be bad news for body image – even if you think you look super hot. That's because when you focus too much on your appearance, you can forget about all the other ways your body is brilliant.

To explain more about this, I'm going to hand over for a second to Dr Nadia Craddock, who has a really cool job researching how people feel about their bodies.

Positive body image is more than liking how you look. It's about appreciating your body for what it allows you to do, respecting and looking after your body, accepting your body, and feeling at home and connected with it.

Dr Nadia Craddock

Some people call this body esteem. You've probably heard of self-esteem – it's the type of word grown-ups throw around a lot. Well, body esteem is kind of similar. It's really important if we want to feel good and live our lives to the full. Having good body esteem means focusing on what your body can DO and not on how it looks.

It means enjoying fun things, like zooming down a hill on your bike or laughing so hard you feel you might burst, without worrying about what your body looks like while you're doing these things.

When we feel bad about our bodies, we are less likely to treat them with kindness and more likely to miss out on cool experiences. If you've ever had a day when you felt bad about your body, I want you to know that this is really common. Lots of people feel this way sometimes, and you can't tell what someone's body image is just by looking at them. Even celebrities with millions of followers can have bad body-image days.

Sam Smith is an award-winning singer and songwriter from the UK who has used their platform to normalize conversations about body image.

Every holiday I've ever been on where [. . .] I had to take my T-shirt off and get in the pool was a painful experience for me. [. . .] But on one holiday I thought, *I'm going to need to fight this because I can't live my life like this any more.*

Sam Smith

Being worried about their body (or having bad body esteem) stopped Sam from diving in the pool. But realizing that their body image was getting in the way of them enjoying life helped them to overcome those difficulties and start focusing on the important stuff – like having fun on holiday.

TUNING IN TO YOUR BODY

You might have wondered what Dr Nadia meant by 'feeling at home' with your body. Well, it's all about feeling comfortable in yourself. One way to do this is by tuning in to your body, which has nothing to do with musical instruments and everything to do with learning to understand what your body is telling you.

The process of tuning in to your body is called **interoception**. It is how you perceive the senses and feelings within your body – in other words, how you speak your body's language. There are lots of ways your body talks to you every single day.

Your stomach might rumble when you're hungry.

You might get butterflies in your belly when you're nervous.

You might feel like you're about to burst if you're desperate for the toilet.

All of these signals are ways your body tells you what it needs. By listening and responding to these messages, you can learn how to look after your body.

There are lots of reasons why you might ignore what your body is saying. For example, you might be so absorbed in a task that you don't even feel your stomach rumbling. But research has shown that bad body image can weaken the connection with these signals, so that you notice them less and less. The noise of body anxiety can stop you from hearing your body's messages, a bit like when you're bopping along to your headphones and don't hear a grown-up shouting,

DINNER!

Bad body image doesn't just affect your **mental health** – it affects your whole body too.

Being tuned in to your body means you're more likely to just live your life and enjoy how your body feels doing stuff than you are to worry about how it looks. This is called **embodiment** (not to be confused with the Ancient Egyptian embalming process involving mummies, bandages and pyramids).

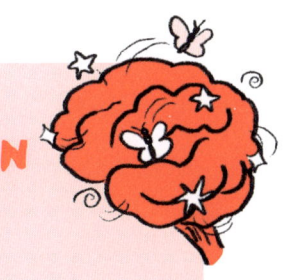

WHEN INTEROCEPTION IS TRICKY

It's worth remembering that everyone's brain works in different ways. This is called **neurodiversity**. Some of us will find it harder than others to interpret our bodies' signals. For example, sometimes people who are **neurodivergent** can find interoception difficult. So, if you're reading this and realizing you have to work harder to listen to your body, or that some of the regular sensations you feel in your body are actually really uncomfortable, that's not a bad thing. It just means your brain might work a bit differently, in the same way that some people find maths easier and others prefer drama or PE.

BUT WHERE DOES BAD BODY IMAGE COME FROM?

To answer this question, the first thing you need to learn is this:

BODY IMAGE
IS NOT A
'ME' ISSUE.

IT'S A
'WE' ISSUE.

Bad body image comes from harmful attitudes in society that affect **everybody**. Whether it's all the princesses in cartoons having thin waists, or superheroes always showing off their muscles, or the way villains in stories are described with crooked teeth, ideas about how we 'should' look are everywhere. And this is no coincidence, because bad body image makes money.

Let me explain. The health and beauty industries are worth **billions** of dollars, and in order for companies to keep making more money they need us to buy more and more stuff. And one way to guarantee that customers keep coming back is to make them feel like there is something (or lots of things) wrong with their bodies. From pills that promise to make us look a certain way to books and clubs telling us exactly what to eat and how, these industries thrive on making us feel our bodies aren't good enough –

then selling us a solution to 'fix' the 'problem'. And it's not only the health and beauty industries that are to blame. Films, TV, fashion and adverts for everything from underwear to cleaning products all sell us a very limited idea of what a 'beautiful' body looks like.

So it's no surprise that lots of us feel like we need to change how we look. This is called

APPEARANCE PRESSURE.

And guess what? Even adults aren't immune to it. In fact, sometimes adults are part of the problem, because the way they talk about their bodies – and yours – can also affect your body image.

BODY FACT

Children in higher-weight bodies are 63% more likely to be bullied.

Appearance pressure doesn't just affect how we think and feel about our own bodies. It can affect how we think and feel about other people's bodies too. Treating someone badly because they have a higher-weight body is a form of bullying known as **weight stigma**, and it comes from appearance pressure telling us which bodies are good and which are bad. Appearance pressure is bad news for everyone, because when people feel anxious about their own bodies, they can be more likely to judge other people's bodies too.

And that's another reason why body image is a 'we' issue. When people are struggling with appearance pressure, or hold ideas about what good or bad bodies look like, it can lead them to make unhelpful or even mean comments. That in turn affects our own body image. So even if we work really hard to feel happy in our own bodies, the way people act around us can still affect how we feel. It's not a problem we can just solve by ourselves.

HOW CAN I CHANGE HOW I FEEL ABOUT MY BODY?

One way of changing how you react to appearance pressure is by practising **body appreciation**. This means focusing less on how you look and more on how your body lets you enjoy life. Maybe your body allows you to beat your brother on the Xbox, nail a yoga pose or bake the perfect brownies? All the things you love to do wouldn't be possible if it weren't for the body you have. Without it, you'd just be a ghost floating about in the air!

THREE WAYS TO SUPERCHARGE YOUR BODY APPRECIATION

1 IMAGINE YOU'RE SPEAKING TO YOUR BEST FRIEND

If your friend said something mean about their own body in front of you, what would you tell them? It might help to think of the top three things you love most about your best friend, then think about the things they might say they love about you. I'm betting the way you look isn't on that list, right?

2 WRITE YOUR BODY A THANK-YOU NOTE

Don't worry, this is nothing like those boring birthday thank-you notes you have to write to all your relatives. This is a chance for you to think about the things you'd like to thank your body for today. It could be for scoring an awesome goal, acing a maths test or giving your friend a great hug.

(Note: unlike birthday thank-you notes, body thank-you notes work best when done more than once a year!)

3 USE POSITIVE AFFIRMATIONS

Scientists have found that when we speak positively to ourselves we turn on a part of the brain called the reward centre – the bit that lights up when you have a happy experience. If you talk or write about appreciating your body, your brain will naturally think about it in a more positive way. The fancy name for this is a **positive affirmation**. Some of my favourites are:

My body can do AMAZING things.

My body is a MIRACLE.

My body WORKS HARD FOR ME.

You can have those ones for free. Now, which ones will you add?

You can tell yourself positive affirmations while you look in the mirror, write them down in a notebook or turn them into a piece of art.

MY BODY IS A MIRACLE

BODY-MYTH ALERT: To have a positive body image, you have to like your body every second of every day.

Do you like your best mate all the time? Even when they're talking about something you find seriously boring? What about your dad when he's nagging you to tidy your room? My point is, loving someone or something doesn't mean you have to like them every single second of every single day.

Body image is a fluid thing. It changes, just like our bodies. We are human beings, not pieces of plastic. Our bodies grow and develop throughout our lives, and the way we think and feel about them can change from one day to the next too. Accepting that you *don't* have to adore every inch of yourself all the time is actually pretty powerful. This attitude is known as

BODY NEUTRALITY.

This is the idea that you can appreciate and care for your body while also knowing that it's not the most important thing about you. Some people also like to use the term

BODY ACCEPTANCE,

which means accepting your body just as it is.

The point is, you don't have to love your body all of the time. You can be angry with it, confused by it or indifferent towards it, and that's **one hundred per cent OK**.

We might not be always happy with our bodies, and we might sometimes mess up and make judgements about other people's bodies, but we can all learn from these moments and do better in the future. Body neutrality or body acceptance can help us deal with these moments and hopefully experience fewer of them.

You might find this hard when people are always commenting on your appearance. Adults just can't seem to stop themselves from pointing out when you've grown loads or got a new haircut, can they?! But, whatever Aunty Wendy might think about your hair, remember that your body is important because it's *yours* – and other people's opinions can't change that.

We are all so much more than our bodies. In fact, when you really think about it, our bodies are kind of the least interesting thing about us. Imagine having an hour long conversation about your little toe or your elbow. Actually, maybe you should try that next time Aunty Wendy comments on how much you've grown . . .

SO WHAT CAN WE ALL DO ABOUT BAD BODY IMAGE?

We know that poor body image is a societal issue. That means that everyone in society has a responsibility to create change, so that everyone feels like their body is good enough exactly as it is.

I know what you're thinking:
I have enough to do keeping up with my homework, my friends, Netflix . . . I don't have time to change the world!

I hear you. I know you are very busy. But remember that you are not alone in this. Not only are other people feeling a similar way, but there's a whole world of people out there coming together to do something about it. And if we all play our part, change will happen faster.

What do you think might happen if more people knew that *all* bodies are *good* bodies? What if everyone knew the problem wasn't their body, but the culture that taught them to view it as bad?

THE SOLUTION TO EVERYONE FEELING BETTER IN THEIR BODY IS TO CREATE A WORLD WHERE **ALL BODIES ARE APPRECIATED AND RESPECTED.**

And, in this book, you're going to find out how you can be a part of that change. It can start in your school playground, your group of friends or a single conversation with a family member. But first, we're going to dive into some of the science and history behind why every body is

UNIQUE AND WORTH CELEBRATING.

CHAPTER 2
ALL BODIES

One certainty about humans is that our bodies are ALL different. There are fat bodies, thin bodies, tall bodies, short bodies and many more in between. This variety is called **body diversity** and it's a wonderful thing.

Did you wince when I used the word **'fat'** to describe one type of body just then? 'Fat' is often used as an insult and seen as something negative, when in fact it's simply a neutral descriptor, like **'tall'** or **'short'**. **'Fat'** isn't a bad word. However, it's also important to remember it is not your place to comment on someone else's body. The words you use to define your own body are your choice, and the same goes for the person next to you. When you comment on someone else's body, you take that choice away from them.

WHAT DOES BODY DIVERSITY ACTUALLY MEAN?

Body diversity describes the ways our bodies are all different – not just in the way they look, but in the way they function too. This is why your best mate might be taller or shorter than you, or you might have classmates who have super-fast fingers on their games consoles while others find it much harder, or who are pros at wheelchair basketball while others struggle to catch the ball. This is normal.

BODIES ARE **NOT** ALL MEANT TO BE THE SAME.

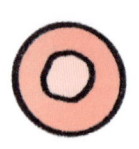
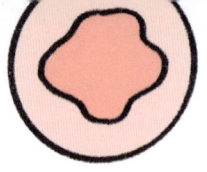

THE SCIENCE PART

Before you were born, you existed as a single cell. Around nine months later, when you were born as a human baby (or a bit earlier if you were born prematurely), your body was made up of lots of different cells – around twenty-six billion, to be exact!

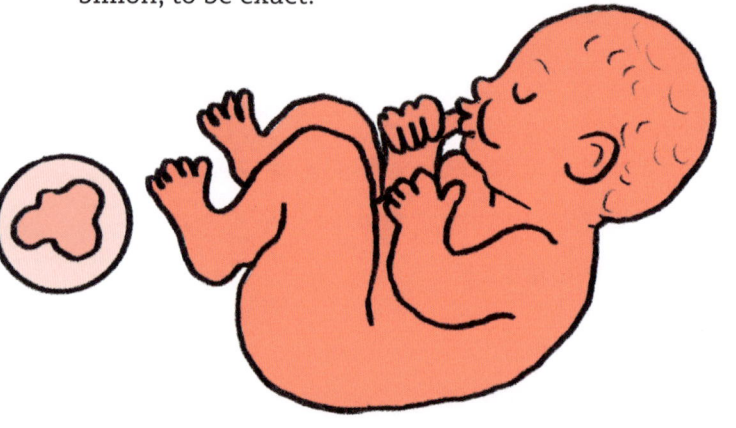

These cells are the building blocks of our bodies. Each cell in the human body contains genes, which are made up of something called **DNA**, which in turn is basically the instruction manual for your body. DNA is a bit like the code in a video game. It's responsible for building and maintaining your body, and it's something that every living thing on planet Earth has – even the tiny weeds in the cracks in the pavement.

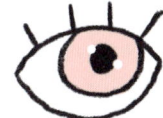

Genes are short sections of DNA that control certain things about the body, like whether a person has blue eyes or brown eyes. Our genes come from our biological parents so, while our DNA and genes are all different, the more closely related we are to someone, the more similar their DNA will be to ours. This is why you might look similar to your biological brother or sister, or why Great-uncle Bill might get you confused with your mum.

*(***Note:*** *all families are different, and many children don't live in families that they are biologically connected to. If that's you, you'll already know your family is just as valid and important as any other. Our families are just another way we are different from one another.)*

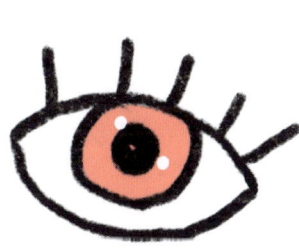

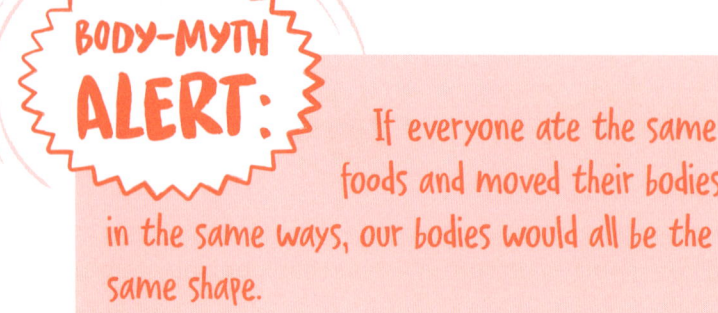

BODY-MYTH ALERT: If everyone ate the same foods and moved their bodies in the same ways, our bodies would all be the same shape.

You know how the thermostat in your house controls when the radiators turn on and off? Well, your body is kind of similar. We all have an internal thermostat, and it's called our set point. It has nothing to do with the temperature in your living room, but instead controls the point at which your body weight goes up or down. Your set point is determined by your genes. And since your genes are inherited from your biological parents, you may find that you have a similar body shape to them when you grow up.

This is why, even if we all ate exactly the same foods and moved our bodies in exactly the same ways, we would still all have different-shaped bodies. We are genetically programmed that way. It's science!

BODY FACT:

Humans started evolving diverse body types around 1.7 million years ago.

Until fairly recently, many experts assumed ancient humans were all pretty much the same height and weight. But we now know this wasn't true. Archaeologists from the University of Cambridge, in the UK, discovered that humans started evolving a range of body types around 1.7 million years ago, back when sabre-toothed tigers and woolly mammoths were around. So the idea that human bodies should all look the same isn't just misguided – it's against evolution.

HOW BODIES ADAPTED TO BE DIFFERENT

We know that our genes decide things like our skin, eyes, hair and body shape. But – and this is the interesting bit – these things can also be influenced by our environment. If we go back to the very olden days (even before the 1990s, when I was a kid), we start to understand why humans are not all made to be the same.

Our ancestors' body shapes changed over a really long period of time – around 40,000 years to be precise! – so that they gradually became better at surviving in their environment.

Humans living in cold climates developed shorter, stockier builds in order to retain the heat better and therefore keep warm.

Meanwhile, humans living in hotter countries adapted to be darker-skinned to help protect their bodies from absorbing the sun's harmful UV rays.

In the extremely cold regions of northern Asia and the Arctic, people developed broader, flatter face shapes to reduce the effects of frostbite.

And humans living in places that got less sunlight throughout the year developed blue eyes, which some scientists think may be better adapted to shorter, darker days.

Although we may no longer need these characteristics in the modern world (where, thankfully, we're not shivering in caves or running away from sabre-toothed tigers), human history shows how we've ended up with an amazing variety of physical appearances. It's pretty awesome, don't you think?

BODY-MYTH ALERT: You can tell how healthy someone is just by looking at them.

This particular myth comes from the idea that someone in a fat body can't be healthy, which is an example of **anti-fat bias**. Similar to weight stigma, anti-fat bias means treating people badly because of their size, and making judgements and assumptions about fat bodies. This includes the idea that, if someone is fat, it must be because they are eating the 'wrong' foods or not moving their body in the 'right' ways.

(**Side note:** *there's no wrong way to eat, and no right way to move your body – but we'll get into that later.*)

As we've just learned, our body shape is affected by lots of things we can't control, from our genes to the type of environment our great-great-great-great-(keep on saying 'great' for a few more hours) grandparents lived in. Society places a lot of emphasis on weight as a sign of how healthy someone is, but this ignores body diversity and the fact that

DIET AND EXERCISE ARE NOT THE ONLY THINGS THAT AFFECT SOMEONE'S BODY SHAPE.

There are plenty of incredible athletes, artists and performers who are challenging this narrow view of what a healthy body looks like.

Trina Nicole is a dancer and founder of the UK's first plus size dance class: The Curve Catwalk. She has performed alongside artists including Nao, Lizzo and Beyoncé, is an ambassador for Nike London and has fronted campaigns for Gap, Clarks, British Vogue and Simply Be. Trina uses her platform to champion body inclusivity and diversity both on and offline.

I'm more than happy to refer to myself as 'plus-size' but, at some point, we need to move away from the label and be neutral to be seen as a human. Why can't I just be seen as a dancer? Why do I have to be a plus-size dancer? That's already making someone seen as 'other'.

Trina Nicole

BODY-MYTH ALERT: All disabilities are visible.

Body diversity isn't just about the way bodies look. It's also about the way they function. The idea that you can tell whether or not someone is disabled simply by looking at them ignores the fact that not every **disability** will have a physical sign, because all bodies function differently. There are lots of different ways for a body to exist, and lots of different ways to be disabled. For example, you may be blind and require a screen-reader to use a phone, or you may be Deaf and communicate using sign language. Some people have hidden disabilities, also known as invisible disabilities, which don't show up in how a person looks. A hidden disability can be physical, mental or neurological (meaning it affects the brain or nervous system).

When someone is disabled, it means the world hasn't been designed for the way their brain or body works. Someone who needs a wheelchair to get around can't use spaces that have lots of stairs but no wheelchair ramps. This is an example of inaccessibility.

The **social model of disability** tells us that it is our inaccessible society that disables people, because it puts up barriers that make life harder for disabled people. These barriers can be physical, like inaccessible changing rooms, or they can be caused by people's attitudes towards those with different needs These are examples of **ableism**, which is a form of discrimination against disabled people.

The world can be inaccessible in many ways. Assuming that disabled people are all wheelchair-users is an ableist point of view. Disability **activists** like Haben Girma campaign for a more **accessible** and equal world where disabled people aren't limited by their environment.

Haben Girma is an American disability rights lawyer, author and public speaker. The first Deafblind person to graduate from Harvard Law School, Haben was named by former US president Barack Obama as a White House Champion of Change.

It's a sighted, hearing classroom in a sighted, hearing school in a sighted, hearing society. They designed this environment for people who can see and hear. In this environment, I'm disabled. They place the burden on me to step out of my world and reach into theirs.

Haben Girma

It's important not to judge how disabled bodies – or any bodies, for that matter – look, particularly because a person's disability can change according to their environment.

THERE IS NOT A ONE-SIZE-FITS-ALL DEFINITION OF DISABILITY.

If in doubt, it's always best to remember that someone else's body is not your business. Instead of expecting disabled people to explain anything about their own bodies, we can all do more to make the world an accessible place for everyone.

HOW TO CELEBRATE ALL BODIES

If you think there's only one 'right' shape or size for bodies to be, you might feel bad if your body doesn't fit the mould. And even if your body *does* fit (or is closer to what we're often told 'good' bodies look like), then thinking that bodies should all look the same can lead you to judge people whose bodies are different from your own.

That's why celebrating body diversity is so important. One way to do this is to make sure you're seeing a range of different body types every single day. You might only see a narrow range of bodies on TV or in the videos you watch online. You might even notice that the toys you used to play with when you were little didn't have many different body types (remember Barbie?!). You can do something about this by seeking out books, YouTube accounts and TV shows that represent a whole range of bodies, not just thin ones. You could look up some of the trailblazers featured in this book for starters. Print off pictures of them to include in a journal. Get posters of them and put them up in your bedroom. (Just don't blame me if they leave Blu-Tack marks on the walls. This was not my idea, OK?!)

WHEN WE START
APPRECIATING ALL BODIES,
WE GET TO SHARE
IN THE UNIQUE
SKILLS, TALENTS AND
KNOWLEDGE OF ALL
KINDS OF PEOPLE -
NOT JUST THE ONES
WHOSE BODIES LOOK OR
FUNCTION A CERTAIN WAY.

But many people are still stuck with out-of-date views on what it means to have a 'good' body. Luckily for them, we're going to talk about this exact subject in the next chapter . . .

CHAPTER 3
GOOD BODY

OK, firstly, can I just say that calling some bodies 'good' and other bodies 'bad' makes no sense. Saying a body is good isn't like when your teacher praises you for good behaviour, or you say 'Good boy!' to your dog because he's fetched a stick. And calling a body 'bad' is just as nonsensical. There is nothing to say that one body is any better or worse than another. Bodies are not either good or bad. They're just . . . existing. You wouldn't look at a skeleton and say, 'Oh wow, that's a good skeleton!' would you?

In fact, *all* bodies are good in the sense that they allow us to live our lives and experience the world. But lots of people will (completely illogically) categorize some bodies as better than others, and this comes from **body ideals**.

WHAT ARE BODY IDEALS?

Body ideals are ways of describing some bodies as good or ideal, and others as bad. Some people also use the term **beauty standards** to refer to how society sets unrealistic expectations for how we 'should' look. These harmful ideals treat body types as things that go in and out of fashion like a style of trainers. What's seen as cool and popular one year won't be the same the next.

The problem with viewing your body in this way is that it's not something you can just go out and buy or forget about when you get bored of it. Unlike the latest TikTok dance everyone is doing or that bag all your mates want, bodies are not a trend or a craze. Your body is the way you experience the world.

THINKING OF YOUR BODY LIKE A JUMPER YOU CAN JUST SWAP WHEN YOU'RE IN THE MOOD FOR SOMETHING ELSE IS REALLY BAD FOR YOUR BODY IMAGE.

'GOOD' BODIES THROUGH THE AGES

The 'ideal' body type hasn't always been the same, and we can see this when we look back at body ideals throughout history. So although body diversity has existed since the days of the sabre-tooth tiger, the type of body that has been celebrated – basically, the one that lots of people think is totally hot – has changed.

LET'S TAKE MEDIEVAL TIMES.

Back then in Europe, most people's lives revolved around the Church, and doctors thought that things like spirits, demons and the position of the stars and planets in the sky determined how bodies worked.
In fact, many doctors wouldn't even treat someone without checking their horoscope first. (To be fair, I know someone who refuses to go on a date without checking the person's star sign, so I'm not judging!) The medieval understanding of bodies was very different from what we know about bodies now.

During this era, rulers and kings were at the top of society's pile, and just beneath them sat knights, who were basically the medieval version of pop stars. But most people didn't have sacks full of cash, so were peasants at the bottom of the pile. Knights were swooned over for being 'athletic' and 'strong', and olden-day books from these times described their 'powerful shoulders' and 'narrow waists'. Kings, meanwhile, showed off their wealth and power by having lavish feasts in their huge castles. A bigger body was seen as a status symbol – a way to show off how much money you had. Take **King Henry the Eighth** (the one with six wives), for instance.

This really isn't my day.

You might have seen paintings of him standing proudly in front of rich tapestries, wearing outfits covered in jewels and fur. His large body in these pictures was meant to show his power and imposing presence. These paintings said to the king's subjects,

'DON'T MESS WITH ME.'

(In case anyone was in any doubt.)

King Henry was the top dude in those days, and the peasants under his rule often didn't get enough to eat. So they tended to associate being fat with being rich and powerful. It was something to aspire to.

(**Note:** it's important to remember here that the amount of food you eat doesn't necessarily determine the size of your body. Remember what we learned about body diversity and genes in the last chapter? Well, none of that was common knowledge – or any knowledge – back then.)

Fashions change, though. What was on trend in Henry the Eighth's time soon went out of style. By the seventeenth and eighteenth centuries, rich people wanted to be thin, because they thought that thinness was proof of their intelligence and their religiousness.

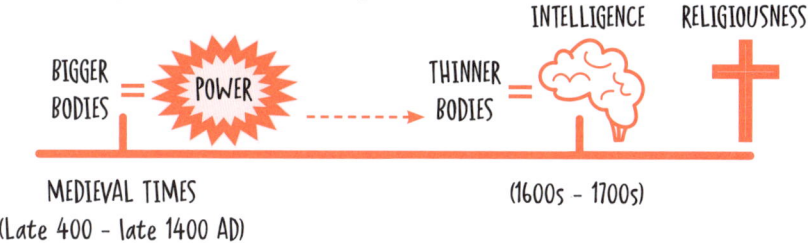

BIGGER BODIES = POWER - - - → THINNER BODIES = INTELLIGENCE RELIGIOUSNESS

MEDIEVAL TIMES
(Late 400 - late 1400 AD)   (1600s - 1700s)

BODY IDEALS AND RACISM

The sociologist and author Dr Sabrina Strings has shown that this trend towards thinness was linked to the transatlantic slave trade, a cruel and inhumane industry in which people from Africa were kidnapped from their homes and taken to European colonies in the Americas, where they were made to work for no money and under terrible conditions. Enslaved people were treated as less than human, and their bodies were seen as objects to be bought and sold. And because Black bodies weren't given any worth in society, the slave trade created a body ideal that said white bodies were 'good' and Black bodies were 'bad'. One sad story that clearly shows this harmful body ideal is that of Sarah Baartman.

Sarah Baartman (also known as Sara and Saartjie, although her birth name is unknown) lived in the country we now know as South Africa in the late eighteenth century. She was a member of the Khoikhoi people, who were among the first people in Southern Africa. When Sarah was sixteen, her husband, a Khoikhoi man, was murdered by Dutch settlers in the country. She was enslaved and sent to Cape Town, where she was forced to work as a servant. Later, she was taken to London, then Paris, and put on show in exhibitions for the entertainment of white people.

The men who enslaved her thought her large bottom and dark skin would make them money, because white people would find her body fascinating. These people didn't think of Sarah as a person, but instead treated her like an animal in a zoo, forcing her to stand on stages wearing barely any clothes while they looked at her body. Sarah was never allowed to go back home, and died in France at the age of twenty-six.

In 2002, nearly 200 years after her death, her body was finally returned to South Africa, eight years after the country's president, Nelson Mandela, made the request.

You can read more about Sarah Baartman on the Kids Britannica website (kids.britannica.com).

Defining a Black person's body as less important or less human than a white person's body was a way for white people in this period to justify slavery. They did this through a made-up, fake science called **race science**.

Race scientists claimed, for example, that Black people were greedy, like animals, with no control over their bodies' desires, while white people were naturally more intelligent and in control of their appetite. Although absolutely none of these ideas are true, many people at the time believed them. Through these racist stereotypes, thinness became linked to whiteness as a way of judging a person's worth.

UNDERSTANDING
THE HISTORY
OF BODY IDEALS
AND WHERE THEY
COME FROM IS
REALLY IMPORTANT.

IT SHOWS US HOW
BODY IDEALS AND
ANTI-FAT BIAS ARE
ROOTED IN RACISM.

Colourism

Another harmful body ideal that stems from the time of slavery is the idea that lighter skin is better or more beautiful.

During this period, pale skin was seen as a sign of goodness, power and wealth. Enslaved people were treated differently according to their skin colour: those with paler skin were often allowed to work indoors, while those with darker skin were made to work outside in the fields. The idea that being paler meant you were somehow 'better' took hold in the communities affected by slavery, and it continued even after the slave trade ended.

This attitude is known as **colourism**.

COLOURISM IS A FORM OF DISCRIMINATION BASED ON SKIN COLOUR. WHEN PEOPLE ARE DISCRIMINATED AGAINST, IT MEANS THEY ARE TREATED UNFAIRLY BASED ON CHARACTERISTICS SUCH AS THEIR RACE, GENDER OR RELIGION. COLOURISM IS WHEN PEOPLE WITH DARKER SKIN ARE DISCRIMINATED AGAINST.

Colourism keeps many parts of the beauty industry in business through the sale of harmful products designed to make dark skin lighter. Even though we now live in a world that looks very different from the one Sarah Baartman lived in, many of the ideals that existed back then continue to affect how people think and feel about bodies and beauty today.

WHAT DO BODY IDEALS HAVE TO DO WITH YOUR BREAKFAST CEREAL?

You may be surprised to hear that the next person I'm going to introduce to the story is the man responsible for the cereal you might have had for breakfast this morning! As well as creating cornflakes and other breakfast cereals, John Kellogg was famous during the nineteenth century in the United States for his views on bodies, health and religion. And he wasn't the only one – his ideas were influenced by Sylvester Graham, the guy behind graham crackers.

Both Kellogg and Graham believed people should avoid anything that made them too excited, including tasty food. This is where their ideas to make plain cereal and crackers came from. As part of the temperance movement, they preached about the benefits to people of giving up things that gave them physical pleasure, including eating certain foods, having warm baths and even sleeping in soft beds. What a pair of mood-hoovers!

People who belonged to the temperance movement believed you could tell how healthy someone was by the shape of their body (which you already know is totally NOT true). They also believed that many illnesses were a punishment from God. They saw having a thin (and white) body as a way to prove how religious and morally good they were.

This movement was an early form of **diet culture**, where people's ideas of 'good' bodies were linked to their ideas about health, religion and what it meant to be a 'good' person.

SPOTTING DIET CULTURE

Diet culture is a set of beliefs that claim you need to have an 'ideal' body (which is not fat) in order to be healthy, popular and successful. These beliefs falsely claim that an 'ideal' body is a thin body. Kellogg and Graham were early promoters of diet culture, and they (falsely) linked body shape to positive personality traits.

Diet culture ignores all the ways our bodies are made to be different. It ignores all the things that influence our health outside of what we eat or how we move our body. Diet culture is not always obvious, because it's all around us. One way to spot it is to recognize when one type of body is being presented as better or ideal. This might show up in the way adults around you talk about health, food or exercise, or in the way an influencer edits their photographs on social media to make their body appear thinner or closer to whatever the body ideal of the moment is.

A quick way to spot diet culture is to ask yourself, 'Am I being encouraged to think of some bodies as good and some as bad?' If the answer is yes, you know there's some invisible diet culture hanging around. Doing this will help you to think critically about what you're being told.

WARNING! *Once you start noticing diet culture, you'll realize it's pretty much everywhere . . . You might even spot it in some of your classes at school.*

FIGHTING BACK AGAINST BODY IDEALS

By the middle of the twentieth century, many people decided enough was enough. They knew that body ideals were making people miserable, and that fat people were being treated badly because of society's ideas about bodies. So they decided to fight back and challenge these ideas. These fat activists created groups such as the National Association to Advance Fat Acceptance (NAAFA) and the Fat Underground, which formed what became known as the fat liberation movement. The aim of this movement was to gain greater **equality** for fat people and it was inspired by other movements of the time, such as the civil rights movement, which fought against racist discrimination.

One famous event in fat-activist history happened in New York's Central Park in June 1967, when five hundred people came together to stage a protest called a Fat In. They carried posters and banners saying things like 'Fat Power', ate snacks, and loudly and proudly shared their stories of being fat. (Sounds like a pretty great protest if you ask me!) This event was an important moment because it forced society to think about how fat people were being discriminated against and to recognize the harm caused by body ideals that said only thin bodies were good bodies.

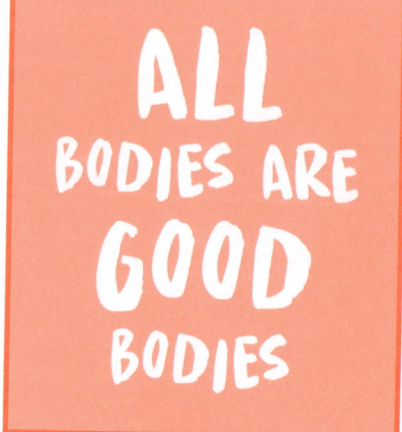

Not all the groups calling for fat liberation agreed on the best way to go about it, though. Some fat activists who were feminists – people who fight for gender equality – felt that the feminist movement needed to do a better job of including fat people. And many people felt that the mainstream fat liberation movement didn't include the voices of Black, queer and disabled women, who were battling multiple forms of discrimination alongside anti-fat bias.

THEIR APPROACH TO CREATING CHANGE WAS **INTERSECTIONAL,** WHICH MEANS THEY UNDERSTOOD THAT PEOPLE COULD BE DISCRIMINATED AGAINST IN MANY DIFFERENT WAYS, NOT JUST FOR THE **SIZE OF THEIR BODY.**

Johnnie Tillmon was a Black feminist activist who, in the United States in the 1970s, campaigned for better welfare for women. (Welfare is also known as benefits in the UK, and refers to the money provided by the government for those who need it or who don't have enough money to live on.) In an important essay, Tilman wrote about all the different ways a Black woman could be discriminated against.

I'm a woman. I'm a black woman. I'm a poor woman. I'm a fat woman. I'm a middle-aged woman. And I'm on welfare. In this country, if you're any one of those things – poor, black, fat, female, middle-aged and on welfare – you count less as a human being. If you're all of those things, you don't count at all. Except as a statistic.

Johnnie Tillmon

Activists continued to make lots of noise through the 1970s, 1980s and 1990s, speaking at conferences and rallies, creating magazines, art and poetry, celebrating fat bodies, and sharing statistics to show how doctors and the medical industry were treating fat people badly. This work all focused on raising awareness of the harms caused by viewing fat bodies as bad bodies.

Judy Freespirit was an American fat activist, co-founder of the Fat Underground group and author of The Fat Liberation Manifesto, a public statement to help people understand the group's aims. The manifesto contained seven points that the group believed, and it is still used as a basis for fat liberation work today. The first point on the list said, 'We believe that fat people are fully entitled to human respect and recognition.'

In the beginning, people giggled when we talked about fat liberation. Now . . . there are hundreds of thousands of fat activists and allies all over the world.

Judy Freespirit

BODY IDEALS TODAY

This leads us nicely to today, and to you, sitting here reading this book. The world that you live in is very different from the past. There are no knights riding around on horses and no cereal inventors telling you to sleep in a hard bed, for starters. And there is also the internet, which has completely changed the way people communicate. Now we can share ideas quickly and easily, look things up at the push of a button, and shout about the things we care passionately about, all without even having to leave the house if we don't want to.

In many ways, the internet has been a really good thing for body image. It's made some of the things that fat activists were fighting for back in the 1960s and 1970s more widely known. But it's also helped to spread body ideals and create unrealistic expectations of how bodies should look.

Body positivity is just about liking your own body.

One thing the internet has given us is the **body positivity movement**, which you might have seen online as

#BODYPOSITIVITY
OR
#BOPO.

This movement is made up of millions of people around the world who are calling for a kinder way to view our bodies. It was started by fat and disabled activists who wanted to create a place to celebrate their bodies and take up space in a world that often told them to be quieter or smaller. Like with anything, though, when lots of people get involved, things get complicated – a bit like when you're playing a game with one friend and ten other people want to join in.

Part of the problem is that many people think body positivity is simply about being positive about your own body. They don't understand that, actually, body positivity means being positive about *all* bodies. If you're positive about your own body but you're not positive about fat bodies or disabled bodies – or any other bodies that don't fit your idea of a 'good' body – then you're not body positive. (This is something to remind the adults around you of too.)

Jade Elouise is an education mental-health practitioner who posts on Instagram as @bodiposipoet.

If you believe that all bodies deserve respect – no matter their shape, size, colour or ability, imperfections or blemishes – then you already have a body-positive mindset.

Jade Elouise

RECOGNIZING YOUR BODY PRIVILEGE

An important aspect of properly understanding body positivity and where you fit into it all is to think about how much **body privilege** you hold. This refers to the size, shape and ability of your body, and the colour of your skin. It also refers to whether you identify with the gender you were assigned at birth (this is called your **gender identity**).

If you hold lots of body privilege, it doesn't mean that you never feel bad about your body, but it does mean that the way you're treated by society might be different from how someone with less privilege than you is treated. There are lots of different ways people can hold body privilege. A fat white person, for example, may be bullied at school because of the shape of their body. But a fat Black person may be bullied for the shape of their body *and* the colour of their skin or texture of their hair.

RECOGNIZING BODY PRIVILEGE CAN HELP YOU TO UNDERSTAND HOW YOU MIGHT EXPERIENCE THE WORLD DIFFERENTLY FROM SOMEONE WITH A BODY THAT'S DIFFERENT FROM YOURS.

Being aware of this will help you to think about how you treat others, and what you can do to make your community a more equal place for everybody.

There are lots of positive ways to use body privilege, but the first step is recognizing it is there.

Knowing that *all* bodies are good, worthy and important bodies sounds simple enough on paper, right? But in reality it can get a bit tricky. That's because there's no end of people ready to tell you otherwise. And when you're a kid and the people telling you to think about bodies as good or bad are adults – maybe even some of the most important adults in your life, like your parents, teachers, doctors or favourite celebrities – well, then it gets really hard.

That's why it might help to think about all the amazing people who've come before you who have fought to change societal attitudes about bodies. They were often laughed at and ignored, but their work and their stories continue to have a huge impact today.

CHAPTER 4

RULES FOR BODIES

You've probably been given lots of rules for your body ever since you were little. Maybe you were told to

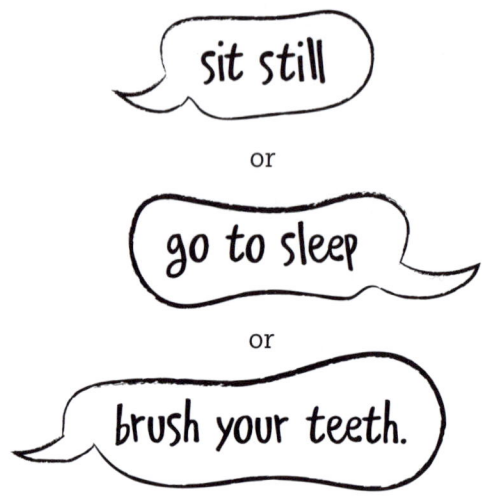

sit still

or

go to sleep

or

brush your teeth.

Rules can be useful, because they can help you to learn how to look after your body. But particularly when they're about eating or exercise, rules for the body can backfire, because they're based on harmful things such as anti-fat bias or a lack of understanding about body diversity. Let's call them Bad Body Rules. (You know I don't like putting the word 'bad' in front of 'body', but I think we can allow it here!)

Remember appearance pressure, which we talked about way back in Chapter 1? Well, it's the reason behind a lot of Bad Body Rules, which tell you that you need to change the way you look to be a better person, or more popular, or healthier, or more successful. The truth is none of these things has anything to do with how you look – but appearance pressure can make it feel that way.

Appearance pressure is one of my least favourite things in the world. I hate it even more than standing on a piece of LEGO® with no socks on. But, even though I hate it, I sometimes find it hard not to fall into the appearance-pressure trap. It can show up in wanting to buy a particular thing, even if I don't need it, because it claims it'll make me look better. Appearance pressure is basically that frenemy who promises you the world, then turns round and steals your favourite pencil when you're not looking.

If you can recognize appearance pressure for what it is, it's easier to stop that sneaky frenemy in its tracks. So we're going to look at where some of these Bad Body Rules come from, and how you can

SAY NO

to them and create your own body rules.

GENDER STEREOTYPES

If we turned to page one of *The Bad Body Rulebook*, it would start with **gender stereotypes**. These are basically the made-up beliefs that say boys are one set of things while girls are another. You know, the ideas that boys are loud and brave, but girls are quiet and kind. That sort of thing.

These stereotypes can lead to **gender norms**, which are unwritten rules for behaving in a particular way based on your gender. For example, only boys should wear blue and play football, while only girls should wear pink and paint their nails. You probably know by now that anyone can paint their nails and anyone can wear blue, but the unwritten rules don't stop there.

BODY-MYTH **ALERT:** Girls are naturally gentle, while boys are naturally strong.

Take the words 'brave' and 'strong', which are often associated with boys. What do 'brave' and 'strong' people look like? Think about Iron Man, Wolverine or Captain America, or even some of the characters on *Fortnite*. They've got big muscles and rippling six-packs. Surrounded by these messages, boys can learn that their bodies are less good if they don't fit this type of image. And, sometimes, a boy might do unhealthy things to try to change the shape of his body so it better fits what he believes a strong, brave body looks like.

Meanwhile, girls are often expected to be 'gentle' and 'kind'. A bit like the princesses in the fairy tales you might have read when you were little, who spent their time singing to birds and befriending lonely dormice. Their kindness and

gentle natures were shown by their flowing hair, narrow waists and big, sparkly eyes. The pressure to look like a gentle princess can impact how a girl feels about her body, just as the pressure to be muscly affects boys.

So one of the first Bad Body Rules that gender stereotypes teach us is:

GIRLS = GENTLE = PRETTY

BOYS = BRAVE = MUSCLY

WRONG!

The unspoken rules continue as we get older. When I was twelve, some older boys made up a mean nickname for me because I had short hair. They'd see me in the corridor and shout:

LITTLE MAN!

That nickname was rooted in another rule, which said I shouldn't have short hair because I was a girl. Maybe you've experienced or witnessed name-calling from other kids based on gender norms?

These narrow gender rules are based on the idea that there are only two ways to exist: either as a boy or as a girl. This is called the **gender binary**, and it leaves out anyone who doesn't fit the mould. While some people will identify with the gender they were given at birth (this is called being cisgender), some may not. The gender binary ignores the fact that there is a whole spectrum of genders. This can mean that those who don't conform to gender norms or to the gender binary – including those who identify as trans, non-binary or gender fluid – can be discriminated against.

Bad Body Rules aren't actually written down in a handbook, but they exist all around us, and can put pressure on us to wear certain clothes, behave in certain ways and think of certain body shapes as better or worse. But here is the truth:

YOU CAN EXPRESS YOUR GENDER IN WHATEVER WAY MAKES YOU FEEL GOOD.

Many of today's biggest stars and fashion icons (including a little-known singer called Harry Styles – heard of him?) are changing up the rules on gender and using style to play around with traditional ideas of masculinity and femininity.

THE **MORE** WE SEE A **RANGE** OF GENDER IDENTITIES REPRESENTED IN TV, FILM AND THE MEDIA, THE CLOSER WE GET TO **BREAKING DOWN** THOSE GENDER RULES.

Yasmin Finney is an actress and TikTok star from the UK who played a trans teen in the hit show *Heartstopper*. In 2023, she made history by becoming the second trans actor to play a starring role on *Doctor Who*.

Hopefully, with the increase of queer-focused projects over the years, the younger generation won't feel pressured to fit a certain mould or live up to society's expectations any more.

Yasmin Finney

HEALTHISM

Another set of Bad Body Rules comes from the way society often defines health. You may have heard some of the adults around you talking about 'being healthy' or 'getting healthy', as if health is this really simple thing you just do, like deciding what outfit to wear in the morning and putting on your favourite pair of jeans.

The idea that our health is all within our own control, and that if we go to the gym or eat lettuce we will automatically 'be healthy', is known as **healthism**. Of course, as we've discussed, what we eat and how we move are not the only things that affect how our bodies look and function. But healthism creates the false idea that there is only *one* way to look 'healthy'. This can lead people to judge bodies that don't follow the 'Bad Body Rules', which may include:

DIETING + EXERCISE = HEALTHY

FAT = UNHEALTHY

THIN = HEALTHY

WRONG AGAIN!

Health isn't a simple set of equations. You can't just add two things together and get a perfect result. There are many other things besides diet and exercise that can affect our health, like where we live and how much money we have to spend on food. But sometimes people think health really is that simple, and assume that someone is unhealthy, or not exercising enough, or eating the 'wrong' kinds of foods, simply because they are in a higher-weight body.

Sometimes, people disguise mean comments about others' weight in questions about their health. This idea of health is based on anti-fat bias. It can even lead to medical weight stigma, a dangerous mindset that means fat patients do not receive the same level of care and treatment as thin patients.

> When fat people are treated badly, their health suffers in all sorts of ways.
>
> **Dr Asher Larmie**

Body rules based on healthism are often disguised as being 'good for your health', but the opposite is true. These Bad Body Rules can cause people to judge others' bodies in ways that can lead to bullying or mistreatment that actually *damages* mental and physical health.

A truly healthy lifestyle is about setting Good Body Rules, which include stuff like brushing your teeth and going to bed at a reasonable time. Not very exciting, I know. Sorry. But health doesn't have to be dull! It can be about finding things you enjoy doing. Things that make you feel good. Perhaps it's a mindful activity, such as journalling or colouring, or a mood-boosting karaoke session, or running around the school playground with your mates. There are so many different ways to take care of your mind and body. Did you know, for example, that laughing is incredibly good for your health? The cheesy phrase that 'laughter is the best medicine' is not wrong:

HA! HA!

HA! HA!

LAUGHTER HAS BEEN SHOWN TO REDUCE STRESS LEVELS AND IT EVEN HELPS TO PROTECT YOUR HEART.

So the next time a grown-up talks about needing to go to the gym to 'get healthy', maybe suggest they try cracking a joke instead.

THE RISE OF THE WELLNESS INFLUENCER

To add to the list of confusing rules surrounding health, there are lots of influencers telling us what to do, eat and buy in order to be 'healthy'. Health or 'wellness' is such a popular topic that it's become its own genre on social media, just like fashion or gaming. On the surface, that's cool. If people want to look at perfectly presented breakfast bowls or gravity-defying yoga poses, then social media is a great place to go. The problem is, much of the wellness advice online is based on healthism, and can give us Bad Body Rules rather than good ones.

Another problem with wellness advice online is that it's often unregulated. This means it isn't checked by anyone, so it isn't always based on proper scientific evidence. Even if the advice does have some science behind it, it might only use sources that back up the influencer's claims and deliberately ignore any evidence that contradicts it. When someone has millions of followers online, people often assume they know what they're talking about – but that's not always the case. And that brings us to our next Bad Body Rule:

MORE FOLLOWERS = BETTER HEALTH ADVICE

WRONG, YET AGAIN!

Although an influencer might be a pro at creating viral videos, this DOES NOT mean they have the expertise to offer health advice. It's a bit like a police officer taking over from your teacher: they may be good at making sure everyone behaves in the classroom, but they don't have the training to know how to teach you stuff like fractions and punctuation.

To make things even more complicated, someone can be an expert in fitness or vegan cooking, but this doesn't mean they are experts in health. Plus, the training that a doctor does is different from the training that a dietitian does, so even a doctor with millions of followers online isn't always the best person to offer food or nutrition guidance. As if that isn't all mind-boggling enough, the field of nutrition isn't very well regulated, which means that someone could do a one-hour online course in nutrition and call themselves a nutritionist. This is obviously different from a person who's studied nutrition at university for many years and has multiple degrees to prove it. And even within the field of nutrition, not everyone agrees about how to approach this stuff.

CONFUSING, ISN'T IT?!

Another big problem with wellness influencers is that some of their advice is culturally appropriated, meaning it has been taken from cultures other than their own. For instance, white wellness influencers may take ancient or sacred practices from Indigenous cultures (practices that, for a time in the past, may have actually been forbidden by white people) and use those practices to make money, all without ever giving any credit to the culture they actually come from.

Annoyingly, like with everything in life, nothing about this is straightforward. Some wellness advice online is useful, and some isn't. We can't throw it all out and say all wellness influencers are bad news, because they're not. What you can do, though, is develop a *wellness radar* – it will help you to spot advice that isn't useful, and separate the Bad Body Rules from the good ones.

Before we do that, though, here are three of the more (ahem) *unusual* wellness trends that have gone viral in the last decade. I one hundred per cent DO NOT recommend trying any of these things at home!

PERINIUM SUNNING. Aka sunbathing your anus. Yes, really. Wellness influencers promoting this have claimed that it increases creativity, aids sleep and helps with concentration. There's absolutely no evidence to show it does any of these things. You do not need to sunbathe your bum!

VAGINAL STEAMING. Promoters of this one have claimed that cleansing the vagina with herb-infused steam reduces stress. FYI, vaginas do not need to be steamed. I repeat: they do *not* need to be steamed.

URINE THERAPY. Drinking wee is as gross as it sounds, and actually really dangerous, despite what some wellness influencers have claimed about it curing allergies. And, in case you're wondering, drinking wee is *never* a good idea.

SPOTTING DODGY WELLNESS ADVICE

Media literacy is a technique that can help you to think critically about everything you read, watch or listen to. It's all about asking questions, and it comes in particularly handy online, when you're trying to sniff out wellness advice that is best ignored.

So the next time you see some wellness content online, ask yourself the following questions.

WHO MADE IT? Is it a person or a company? What do you know about them? Do they have expert knowledge of the topic they are speaking about?

WHY DID THEY MAKE IT? Are they trying to sell you something, or persuade you of something? How does it benefit this person or company to have you watching this content?

WHO IS IT FOR? Is it for kids? Adults? People who have a particular point of view or lifestyle? How can you tell who it's for?

WHAT TECHNIQUES ARE THEY USING TO PERSUADE YOU? Are they using music, attractive images, facts and figures, or scientific language?

WHAT DID THEY MISS OUT? Are they showing both sides of the story? What other relevant information have they not included?

HOW DID IT MAKE YOU FEEL? Are you inspired, shocked, angry, happy? How might this content make someone else feel? Someone whose body doesn't look or function like yours?

There isn't always a right or wrong answer to these questions, and we won't all have the same perspective on something. Having conversations with your family and friends about this stuff may help too, because it can encourage you to listen to other ideas or ways of viewing things.

If you see something online that you find particularly thought-provoking or worrying, then show it to a trusted adult and use these questions to have a chat about it.

THE BEAUTY INDUSTRY

The beauty industry has given us Bad Body Rules for as long as it's existed. And while today's global cosmetics industry is relatively new, the standards it's based on have existed for thousands of years. Did you know, for example, that Queen Cleopatra used vegetable charcoal as eyeliner over 2,000 years ago? Or that, back in the sixteenth century, Queen Elizabeth I covered her face in white lead to hide her smallpox scars? Neither queen could buy her favourite beauty products online like we can now (I'm pretty sure neither whiteleadfacepaint.com nor Vegetable Charcoal for Busy Queens existed back

then), but they still lived by rules that told them they should look a certain way, and they used time and energy to achieve those looks.

Beauty standards may be different these days, but they still exist – and today they are the basis of a huge money-making industry.

BODY FACT:

In 2022, the global beauty market was worth around 430 billion US dollars.

JUST THINK OF ALL
THE COOL THINGS
THAT MONEY COULD
BE SPENT ON!
HOW MANY WHALES,
RAINFORESTS AND
ALMOST-EXTINCT
ORANGUTANS COULD
BE SAVED WITH
$430 BILLION?

The beauty industry gives us Bad Body Rules because it encourages us to spend money fixing 'problems' – such as spots, dimpled skin or frizzy hair – that are actually just normal ways for bodies to be. The industry also tells us that the more money we spend, the better the product will be at solving these problems. And it's not just about buying one expensive product either. Oh no. The beauty industry wants us to spend a lot of time using different products for different steps of our 'beauty routine'. More products mean more money for these businesses. So, the number one Bad Body Rule from the beauty industry is:

MONEY + TIME + LOTS OF PRODUCTS = BEAUTY

Just as healthism has tricked us into thinking its rules for the body are healthy, the beauty industry has tricked us into thinking its rules for the body are about lovely things like self-care and relaxation. Who doesn't love a good pamper, after all? (Ooh, bubble baths! Yes please!) The problem comes when these beauty standards make us feel that our bodies, faces and hair are 'wrong' and, in order to make them 'right', we need to spend loads of money. (By the way, if you want to get some self-care hacks that aren't based on beauty standards then check out the toolkit in the next chapter.)

Many products sold by the beauty industry simply wouldn't exist if we hadn't been made to believe our bodies are problems. Take cellulite, for example. Cellulite is a very normal, natural, harmless and common way for skin to appear. But back in 1968, the beauty industry (for example, *Vogue* fashion magazine) told us that the dimples that show up on lots of people's skin were signs of a 'condition' that needed to be 'cured'. Since then, billions have been spent on anti-cellulite creams invented to supposedly 'cure' us of this very normal, harmless and natural way for skin to appear.

Here are some of the other beauty products that have been sold in recent years. And, no, these aren't made up!

SNAIL GOO. Influencers and beauty journalists have been going ga-ga (or should it be goo-goo?) over creams that contain snail slime. True fact.

BLACKHEAD VACUUM. I wonder if this one comes with lots of different attachments, so you can use it on your carpet too?

WRINKLE IRON. Because why iron your school uniform when you could iron your face? Seriously.

Historically, the beauty industry has targeted women and girls, but these days most beauty brands have products for men and boys too. Beauty standards are shaped by things like reality TV and social-media influencers, and these standards now target everyone. The beauty industry needs us to spend time, energy and money chasing things like sparkly white teeth, smooth skin, bouncy hair and perfectly groomed eyebrows, regardless of our gender. The more time we spend trying to achieve these things, the more money the industry makes.

That's not to say that you shouldn't enjoy beauty products like make-up if they interest you. (And if you're at the age where the grown-ups in your life let you buy them . . . I wouldn't advise borrowing Aunty Wendy's glittery eyeshadow. She might get very annoyed!) Like fashion, make-up can be an awesome way to express your creativity. And if you have zero interest in any of this, then that's also cool.

THE IMPORTANT
THING IS THAT YOU
SHOULD NEVER FEEL
LIKE YOU NEED TO
'FIX' ANYTHING
ABOUT YOUR BODY -

YOU ARE **UNIQUE**
AND **WONDERFUL**
JUST AS YOU ARE.

YOUR BODY, YOUR RULES

Now, I'm not going to tell you how to think or feel about your body. There are enough body rules around already, and I certainly don't want to add to them. Along with all the Bad Body Rules telling you how your body should look, there are also rules telling you how you should feel about it. It's almost as if you can't win: you're either expected to try to change your body and live up to appearance pressure, or you're expected to love every inch of your body and shout about it at the same time (which just adds another kind of pressure if you end up feeling as though you're 'failing' at having a positive body image).

YOUR BODY IS NOT MY BODY. IT IS YOURS, AND YOURS ALONE.

Your body is the most precious thing you will ever own. It lets you experience the world and live the life that you have. And, because it's yours, that means that only *you* get to be in charge of it.

I'm hoping that, as you're reading about body image and uncovering the many parts of the story that shape how you (and I, and everyone else with a body) feel about bodies, you'll realize you have a lot to gain by being kind to your body and the bodies of those around you. But whatever you decide and whatever you choose to believe, the only real body rule you need to take with you through life is this:

YOUR BODY, YOUR RULES.

Remember that next time a wellness influencer tells you to drink wee.

CHAPTER 5

RESPECTED BODY

Have you ever played *Animal Crossing*? It's a computer game where you get to design your own virtual island. If you don't log in for a while, virtual weeds grow. They look harmless, like grass, but if you're not careful they can grow everywhere and affect your rating on the game. Diet culture is like those harmless-looking weeds. It might seem like no big deal on the surface, but if you're not careful it takes over and changes the way you think about your body and how you treat it. It can also affect how you think about other bodies, and how you act towards people whose bodies don't look or function like your own.

While the weeds on *Animal Crossing* disguise themselves as grass, diet culture disguises itself as health. This may sound familiar – as we learned in the last chapter, healthism uses the same sneaky disguise. Diet culture, healthism and appearance pressure are all part of the same problem, and can make us do unhealthy things to fit in with a narrow version of what 'healthy' should look like.

In this chapter, we're going to talk more about diet culture, which covers society's general attitudes towards health and bodies, and the pressure that is put on us to look a certain way. Most importantly, we're going to learn how to look after and respect our bodies without falling for diet culture's tricks.

But before we do that, we need to understand a bit more about health in general.

THE HEALTH JIGSAW PUZZLE

Health is really complicated. There are many things out there – some of which you might never have thought about before – that have an impact on your health. It's a bit like a huge jigsaw puzzle, with lots of different parts of your life as the pieces. They're all important, and you can't complete the puzzle if even one piece is missing.

Here are some of the pieces to keep in mind.

🧩 PUZZLE PIECE 1: Your environment

Did you know that your health can be affected by where you live? If you live somewhere with lots of pollution, for example, you are more likely to develop asthma. Meanwhile, if your home is cosy and warm with no mould or damp, you're less likely to experience asthma, allergies or other breathing problems related to housing issues.

This is one example of something called the **social determinants of health**. This sounds complicated, but it simply means that a collection of things affect your health: where you live, whether you have access to education, whether you can see a doctor when you're ill and whether your family can afford to buy food.

BODY FACT:

In 2022, it was reported that four million children in the UK lived in households that had struggled to afford to buy food.

PUZZLE PIECE 2: Your relationships

The way you're treated by other people and the relationships you have with your friends, family and classmates have an effect on your health too. If you're bullied, for example, it can make you stressed, sad, depressed and anxious. This puts a strain on your nervous system, which sends messages all over your body, and it can suffer from wear and tear, just like that old toy you loved as a toddler. So, because things like bullying and discrimination can affect your nervous system, they can also have a physical impact on your body.

Meanwhile, the happy relationships you have with people you love are good for your nervous system. Friendships are kind of like the nervous system's equivalent of a soft, cosy blanket on a freezing cold day. These relationships make you feel good, which is good for your physical and mental health.

PUZZLE PIECE 3: Your genetics

Hopefully you remember from Chapter 2 how diversity is built into the human species, and how our genetic make-up (the DNA kind, not the eyeshadow kind) influences the way our bodies look and function. For example, you may have been born with a pre-existing allergy, illness or condition that affects your health. Or your genetics may mean you are more likely to develop a condition later in life that has an effect on your health.

This is why it's so harmful to assume that health is all within a person's individual control. It's an idea that can lead to people being judged or discriminated against simply because of the genes they were born with.

 PUZZLE PIECE 4: Your health behaviours

Health behaviours are things you do to look after your health. These are the Good Body Rules that we talked about in the last chapter, and they're the one piece of the puzzle that you have a little bit of control over. I say 'a little bit' because your health behaviours will also be affected by the environment you live in, your relationships and your genetics. The puzzle pieces are all linked!

Despite what diet culture says, health behaviours are about much more than eating veg or moving your body. Drinking enough water is a health behaviour, and so is wearing sun cream. (You may think your fave celeb looks totally hot with a tan, but I promise you there is nothing hot about sunburn – except that you feel, well, actually hot.)

THREE THINGS TO REMEMBER ABOUT HEALTH BEHAVIOURS

There are lots of different types of health behaviours.

IT'S NOT JUST ABOUT WHAT YOU EAT OR HOW YOU MOVE YOUR BODY. HEALTH BEHAVIOURS ARE AS DIVERSE AS BODIES ARE.

HEALTH BEHAVIOURS ARE FOR EVERYBODY, REGARDLESS OF WHAT THEIR BODY LOOKS LIKE OR HOW IT FUNCTIONS.

HEALTH BEHAVIOURS ARE ABOUT LOOKING AFTER YOUR BODY, NOT TRYING TO CHANGE THE WAY IT LOOKS.

Interestingly, researchers have found that people with positive body image are more likely to have healthy behaviours. They're also less likely to do dangerous things that risk their health, like smoking or trying out a restrictive diet that sees them counting calories or following rigid food rules. Basically, the more connected and at home you are in your body, the easier you'll find it to do things that make your body feel good.

BUILDING NEW HEALTH BEHAVIOURS (AKA HEALTHY HABITS)

If you're trying to make a new health behaviour part of your regular routine, you're probably going to have to do it quite a bit before it becomes a habit. Just like learning a new instrument – or developing any new skill – the more you do it, the easier it gets.

BODY FACT:

It can take a person anything from 18 to 254 days to form a new habit.

Scientists have found it can take a while to form a new habit, and the length of time is not the same for everyone. For example, say you decided you wanted to get a bit more sleep every night. Your new healthy habit might involve turning off the TV or your phone and getting into bed earlier, then reading or journalling for a while before going to sleep. Statistics show that, on average, you will need to do your new bedtime routine for sixty-six days (that's just over two whole months!) before it becomes automatic.

To get your new habit to stick, you could try the following things.

- Write your new routine down and stick it on the wall to remind yourself what to do.

- Create a visual routine with pictures. This can help if you are neurodivergent or struggle with **executive functions**, which can make planning and time management difficult.

- Set an alarm to remind yourself when it's time for bed.

- Set screen-time limits on your phone, if you have one.

All this has nothing to do with being a kid, by the way. I'm a fully grown adult and I still have to do all these things, because apparently you never grow out of wanting to stay up too late!

A final thing to remember when you're thinking about introducing a new healthy habit is to

SET SMALL, ACHIEVABLE GOALS.

This might mean bringing your bedtime forward by half an hour at first, instead of a whole hour. (Across a week, that will still amount to three and a half extra hours of sleep!) Smaller goals make it easier to build new habits that leave your body feeling good and that don't feel like chores (because, let's be honest, no one needs more chores in their life).

And don't forget to celebrate your achievement of building a new habit with a reward! My personal favourite is a movie afternoon with snacks, a fluffy blanket and the curtains closed, but that's just me.

A health behaviour that feels good for one person might not be the same for another. Our bodies are all different, so what our bodies need is often different too. Your best friend might need eleven hours of sleep a night to feel good, whereas you might be able to function perfectly well on nine. Or you might notice the label on your favourite food says something about how many calories a person should consume every day. These rules and labels don't take into account the ways our bodies are all different. You might need to eat more or less than your best friend to feel full and to have enough energy – and that's OK!

THERE'S NO SINGLE RULE FOR BODIES OR HEALTH BEHAVIOURS.

LOOKING AFTER YOUR MENTAL HEALTH

Have you ever worried about something and got a tummy ache? Or been mega excited and found it hard to fall asleep? Or maybe you've had an argument with a friend and it's made you lose your appetite or feel a bit sick? This is because your mind and body are connected. So when you experience an emotion or feeling, it's likely to show up as a physical sensation in your body.

You've probably heard the term **mental health** lots already. But do you really know what it means? Mental health includes your emotional, psychological and emotional well-being. We all experience different emotions, thoughts, feelings and moods throughout a day, week and year. This is normal. We can't be jumping up and down with happiness every second of every day. But things get difficult when the emotions that feel challenging become too much to cope with.

Some of the ways poor mental health may show up are:

- feeling worried a lot of the time, to the point where you struggle to sleep, eat and go to school or hang out with your friends

- having problems eating and a difficult relationship with food

- feeling sad a lot of the time and not wanting to get out of bed or leave the house

The way we think and feel about our bodies is important to our overall physical and mental health. When we struggle with poor body esteem, it can affect our physical and mental health in lots of different ways. It can make us feel anxious, depressed or sad. And it can stop us from doing things that will make us feel good, such as hanging out with our friends, moving our bodies or going outside.

Many mental health campaigners argue that mental health should just be called health, and given as much attention as physical health because it's equally important. It doesn't exist in a separate room somewhere in your body.

YOUR MENTAL HEALTH IS A PART OF YOU, AND IT AFFECTS EVERY BIT OF YOU.

Dr Tosin Ajayi-Sotubo is a GP based in the UK, with a passion for spreading mental health awareness.

> Just like our physical health, our mental health is something that we all have and, in the same way we look after our physical health, we need to take care of and look after our mental health too.
>
> Dr Tosin Ajayi-Sotubo

Looking after your mental health is called mental wellness, or mental fitness, and it's all about finding ways to look after your mind so that your thoughts, feelings and emotions don't become too hard to cope with. One way of doing this is to regularly make space in your life to do things that you love. It also helps to have a toolkit to draw on when things feel difficult.

YOUR SELF-CARE TOOLKIT

Self-care is about way more than avocado on toast or bubble baths. In fact, before self-care was used to sell posh creams and candles, it was a concept used by civil rights activists to look after their communities. And, before that, it was used by doctors in the 1950s to help patients to find ways to look after their health outside the hospitals.

You can be kind to yourself without feeling like you must have all the stuff your favourite wellness influencer is selling. So here are some totally free ways you could create your own self-care toolkit.

1 NAME THE FEELING

Did you know that naming an emotion can help take the sting out of it? Neuroscientists have found that our brains automatically feel better when we name a feeling. Sometimes, we're so caught up in the feeling itself we're not even sure what it is. To make things even more confusing, you might be experiencing more than one emotion at the same time. Learning to identify and name your feelings can be a useful step to feeling better.

So next time you're wrapped up in a feeling, see if you can take a second to ask yourself,

> What is the emotion that I'm experiencing?

And then send a clear signal to your brain by naming the emotion. Say to yourself,

> I am feeling sad/stressed/anxious/[insert feeling here].

❷ TALK ABOUT IT

Talking about your feelings can be another important step in working through them. Sometimes, adults will try to make everything better and rush to give advice without really listening to you. Although they mean well, this isn't always helpful. If this happens, it might help to write a note for them beforehand. Something like:

> I need to talk to you.
> Can you promise to really listen while I'm talking, without trying to give an answer first?

Talking about your feelings might make you uncomfortable, in which case going for a walk and having a chat along the way can help. There's some evidence to suggest that being shoulder to shoulder with someone rather than face to face can help us to open up if we're struggling to find the words.

③ WRITE IT DOWN

If talking isn't your thing (or even if it is), writing your feelings down can help too. You don't need a fancy journal to do this – scrap paper is fine. Some people also like to list the things they're worrying about, then give themselves a specific time in the day to think about them. This is called a Worry Window. Maybe you could write down the things that are bothering you, then take that list to talk through with someone you trust?

④ MOVE THE FEELING AROUND

Movement can help to reduce the impact of stress, anxiety, anger and other feelings. It doesn't have to be a five-mile run. Jumping up and down on the spot, waving your arms in the air or having a kitchen disco all work too! There's science behind this. When you're anxious, your body releases a hormone called adrenaline. This is your body's 'fight or flight' response, which was useful when our ancestors had to run away from sabre-toothed tigers but is less so now. Moving your body can help to reduce the impact of that adrenaline and give your brain a clear signal that it's safe.

🄯 GIVE YOURSELF A HUG

Our bodies are also designed to seek comfort and reassurance, and for some people that can come in the form of a hug with someone you love who makes you feel safe.

HUGS SEND A CLEAR SIGNAL TO YOUR BRAIN THAT YOU'RE OK.

If you've got no one to hug, or hate hugs with other people, you could just wrap your arms around your body and give yourself a big squeeze. Wrapping yourself up in a blanket and creating a human burrito can also work. (I know it sounds weird, but trust me!)

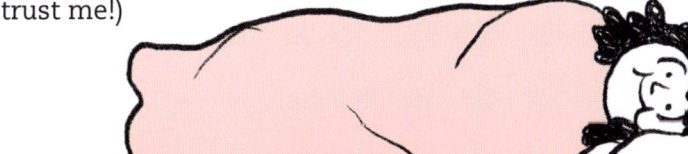

FOOD, GLORIOUS FOOD

I've put off talking about food until now, because traditional health advice is often served up with a massive portion of diet culture. Diet culture makes us think that the only health behaviour that matters is eating certain foods or eating in certain ways, and this advice isn't actually healthy at all.

If you take just one thing away from this chapter, let it be this:

HEALTHY EATING = HAVING A HEALTHY RELATIONSHIP WITH FOOD

Write it down. Say it out loud. Tell your friends. And shout it out to all the adults in your life.

This might be the total opposite of what you've learned about healthy eating up to now. Adults are GREAT at making up rules about food. I know, because I've done it myself in the past, before I knew better.

Jeanette Thompson-Wessen is a fat-positive nutritionist who helps people learn about intuitive eating and have a better relationship with their body.

Food and eating doesn't have to be complicated. Getting a variety of food into what we eat is important to support our health. We don't need to eat in a certain way to be 'healthy'. Food doesn't work like that.

Jeanette Thompson-Wessen

HERE'S THE THING:

HEALTHY EATING
LOOKS DIFFERENT
FOR EVERYONE.

AND, WHEN IT COMES
TO FOOD (YEP, EVEN PEAS),
NOTHING IS MORE
IMPORTANT THAN
YOUR RELATIONSHIP
WITH IT.

A healthy relationship with food looks like:

- eating when you are hungry and stopping when you are full (tell that to Aunty Wendy when she tells you to clear your plate)

- making sure you are eating enough

- acknowledging that food is more than just fuel

- knowing that all foods fit – there is space for all types of food in your diet, from pizza to pineapple and everything in between (as long as you're not allergic, and it doesn't go against your religion)

- not giving food moral value (more on this in a moment!)

- knowing there isn't one single way of eating that fits all people – we all have different nutritional needs, enjoy eating different things, and live in cultures with different foods, and that's OK!

There will be times in your life, times of the year, times of the week when you might find you are hungrier than others. For example, it's totally normal to feel hungrier when you're going through a growth spurt, or studying for a test, or when it's winter and the weather is colder. This is your body telling you that it needs energy from food.

Food is about more than just energy, though. We are human beings, not robots. Your body is not like a car that needs filling up with petrol. Human beings have emotions, thoughts and feelings. We live in cultures that have traditions and celebrations, with food playing an important part in them – just think of all the birthdays where you might have eaten cake.

FOOD CAN BRING YOU COMFORT IN A WAY THAT GOES BEYOND JUST STOPPING YOU FROM FEELING HUNGRY.

THAT'S ABSOLUTELY NORMAL.

IN FACT, IT'S ONE OF THE JOYS OF BEING HUMAN.

You might have heard adults around you talking about some foods as 'good' or 'healthy' and some as 'bad' or 'unhealthy'. This is called giving food moral value, and it's not helpful when you're trying to have a healthy relationship with food. It can make you feel guilt or shame about eating certain foods, or it can mean you develop a fear of certain foods or just avoid them completely. It can also mean you want more of the food that you're told you shouldn't eat. Knowing that all foods fit, that all foods have a place on your plate, is important. You need more than just broccoli, and more than just chocolate, to survive.

What's more, if you're neurodivergent, you might find some eating habits that other people find easy just aren't comfortable for you. You might have a specific list of safe foods that don't make your senses feel overwhelmed, for example. Or there might be times you prefer eating alone. You might sometimes forget to eat because you're so absorbed in a task, or because you don't always notice hunger pangs. Rules about healthy eating can often ignore all the ways we are all different.

Unfortunately, research shows that many children have a difficult relationship with food. For some, this means deliberately limiting the amount of food they eat, and not eating enough to grow, get energy or stop feeling hungry. For others, it can mean regularly eating past the point of comfort. These behaviours might point to a disordered relationship with food, or even an eating disorder.

These two things may sound similar, but there is a difference: disordered eating can be any type of eating pattern that isn't simply eating when you're hungry and stopping when you're full. It could include cutting out a certain food group altogether or going on a strict diet to try to lose weight. These types of behaviours can sometimes lead to an eating disorder, which is a mental illness that can be very dangerous to someone's health. Disordered eating can still have a negative impact on someone's health, even if it does not develop into an eating disorder.

Aya Wingate is an eating disorder dietitian for children and young people.

Sometimes, people start to worry about their eating so much that the idea of eating and how it is going to impact their health and body size becomes overwhelming. If this is something affecting you, it's important you share your worries with family or teachers.

Aya Wingate

If you are struggling with your eating, it's not your fault. It is not something to feel embarrassed or guilty about. It's not something you need to keep secret or to hide. And it's not something you need to cope with alone. If you think you need help with your relationship with food, it's really important to speak to a trusted adult about it.

BODY FACT:

People who diet are more likely to develop an eating disorder.

WHAT TO DO IF YOUR FRIENDS TALK ABOUT DIETING

You might have noticed that some of your friends talk about health, food, bodies and movement in a way that doesn't fit with what you're learning in this book. This can be hard, particularly if you're struggling with the same stuff. It might even feel as though, in order to be a good friend, you have to follow the same rules that your friends have set for their bodies. You do not need to do this.

Your relationship with food is precious, and restricting what you eat to try to change the shape of your body can be very harmful.

You are not being a bad friend for not wanting to join in with your friends' diets. In fact, a good friend would gently let someone know that dieting can be dangerous, and that all bodies are good bodies. You might say something like,

> I've been learning about what it means to have a healthy relationship with food. Maybe this is something that could help you too. Have you talked to an adult about this?

If you're concerned about a friend's relationship with food or the way they are eating (or not eating), then the best thing you can do for them is talk to a trusted adult who can offer support.

PLAYFUL MOVEMENT

Movement is another health behaviour that gets a lot of attention. The problem is, it's not always talked about in a healthy way. (I'm looking at you, #fitspo influencers.)

When you were really little, you moved your body naturally, and did it because of how it made you feel, not how you thought it might make you look.

You might have played and jumped around and danced.

Maybe you wiggled your bum,

or liked to practise balancing.

(If the adults in your life are anything like me, they'll have some super-cute videos of these moments that may now make you cringe.)

THE POINT IS, YOU MOVED YOUR BODY PLAYFULLY BECAUSE IT FELT GOOD. THIS IS HOW MOVEMENT SHOULD ALWAYS BE.

Unfortunately, lots of people think movement is all about looking a certain way, which could be having muscles or being thin. This attitude zaps all the joy out of movement, and means there's nothing playful about it. It also changes people's relationship to movement, so that instead of moving for fun, they choose to exercise because of an extrinsic motivator (any form of motivation or pressure that comes from how exercise makes them look instead of how it makes them feel). It could be anything from a fitness influencer persuading you to try their brand of exercise, to a fitness tracker telling you how many steps you should be doing. And most of this stuff is – you guessed it – just diet culture in disguise. Which can mean that exercise becomes something people dread instead of something they do for fun.

Becky Scott is a British fitness instructor and founder of MissFits Workout, a size-inclusive dance-based workout studio for people who don't feel at home in a gym.

> Once I realized I didn't need to change my body to feel the benefits of exercise, I was able to make it part of my lifestyle – something to look forward to rather than a punishment.
>
> Becky Scott

The good news is that if, like Becky, you can recognize that movement is not about changing how you look, you're more likely to enjoy it and want to do it more often. Researchers have found that, when people move for how it makes them *feel* instead of how it makes them *look*, they tend to do it more consistently. And moving consistently in a way you enjoy is *so much* better for your overall health and well-being than doing something just because a fitness influencer told you to.

Cody Miller is an American Olympic swimmer who was born with a medical condition known as sunken chest syndrome and struggled with body image issues as a boy. Today, Cody shares positive messages from his life as a professional swimmer on his popular YouTube channel.

I distinctly remember not wanting to take off my T-shirt in gym class because I was afraid of getting made fun of . . . Eventually, I gained the self-confidence to grow out of that. My lesson was that everybody has their own insecurities.   Cody Miller

At the same time as challenging stereotypes of how a fitness instructor or athlete 'should' look, people like Becky and Cody are celebrating the joy of movement. And this is important, because movement brings us so many intrinsic benefits that change how we feel *inside* instead of how we look on the outside. Here are just some of the benefits of movement:

IMPROVED **MOOD**

INCREASED SELF-ESTEEM

LEARNING NEW SKILLS

IMPROVED BRAIN, BONE AND LUNG HEALTH

BETTER SLEEP

MAKING NEW FRIENDS.

At this point, you may be wondering why I keep calling it 'movement' instead of 'fitness' or 'exercise'. I like to use the word 'movement' because it helps us to think of all the ways we move our bodies that aren't formal exercise. Some people love organized sport, and some people love PE at school, but not everyone does, and that's OK. There are lots of ways to move around that might not count as formal sport, including:

KITCHEN DISCOS

GOING TO THE PARK

DOING SOME STRETCHING

TIDYING YOUR ROOM

RIDING A BIKE TO YOUR FRIEND'S HOUSE

PLAYING WITH A FRISBEE OR BALL

CHASING YOUR SIBLING
BECAUSE THEY STOLE THE TV REMOTE

SWIMMING.

All of these ways of moving are valid and carry just the same benefits as regular sport does. So, the best way to think about movement without any of the bad vibes of diet culture is to ask yourself this:

WHAT MAKES MY BODY FEEL GOOD?

You might find you're able to concentrate better after you've taken your dog for a walk. Or maybe dancing around with your mates makes you feel happier and more relaxed. There are so many incredible benefits to enjoying free, playful movement – no fancy fitness subscription needed.

CARING FOR YOUR BODY WITH KINDNESS

Now that we've done a deep dive into health and health behaviours, we can start to make a plan for how to care for ourselves with kindness, from a place of respect and love for our bodies.

This is not about making a rule book to follow, but thinking about what will work for you and your life. To help you do this, please allow me to introduce six cheesy quotes which can be your starting point.

❶ NAPS SAVE LIVES

Rest is a really important part of looking after your body. In fact, scientists now believe that getting enough sleep throughout life can actually make people live longer (brilliant justification for a lie-in, if ever I heard one). Sleep is particularly important when your body is growing and changing, and when your brain is working hard to learn and remember new things (hello, school).

Here are some of the benefits of rest, in no particular order:

IT HELPS YOUR IMMUNE SYSTEM.

IT REDUCES STRESS.

IT IMPROVES YOUR ATTENTION SKILLS AND EVEN YOUR MEMORY.

IT CAN BOOST YOUR MOOD.

IT CAN HELP TO REDUCE FEELINGS OF ANXIETY AND WORRY.

On top of your busy school life, it can be easy to fill up your spare time with clubs and activities and forget to make time for rest. (This is something I still struggle with as an adult, to be honest!) It's important to do the things you're interested in, but make sure you leave some time to chill out too. And, when you're resting, make sure you really, properly rest. (No, doing your homework in front of the TV does *not* count as resting.)

Rest doesn't have to be taking a nap. It can also be stretching out on the sofa in front of the TV after a long day at school, having a lovely bubble bath, doing some meditation, or even doodling or colouring.

❷ MOVE TO YOUR OWN GROOVE

Your body needs rest *and* movement – but diet culture often leaves the rest part out of it. Interestingly, lots of the benefits of movement are the same as those of rest: reducing stress, helping you to sleep better, helping with concentration, boosting your mood and helping to reduce anxiety. And, as we just learned, the best approach to movement is to do what makes you feel good, whether it's tap-dancing or tobogganing.

❸ BE KIND TO YOUR MIND

Health behaviours aren't just activities that benefit your body. Your brain is a part of your body too, so don't leave it out. Health behaviours which can be good for your mind include journalling, using positive affirmations, and relaxing activities like bubble baths. (Did I mention those too many times already?)

Setting healthy boundaries for yourself – such as being mindful of how much time you spend on social media, or being able to say no if you feel overwhelmed or don't want to do something – is also important. (I'm not sure this one works with homework, unfortunately, but feel free to show this book to your teacher!)

And perhaps the most important rule for looking after your mind is to talk to someone if you're feeling low.

4 SMELL THE FLOWERS

There's this really cool thing called Blue Mind Theory that describes the relaxed state people can go into when they're on or near water. More recently, scientists have also come up with the term Green Mind Theory, which is all about the health benefits of being in nature. Researchers found that just five minutes of time outside, closer to nature, can have a positive effect on your overall health and well-being.

With this in mind, is there any way you could build a new health habit that means you have a bit more time outdoors each week? Instead of FaceTiming your friend, for example, could you go for a walk together? Or could you walk to school? Or could you take a packed lunch to school some days and eat it outside?

❺ LIFE IS BETTER TOGETHER

One of the hardest things about growing up is the way our relationships change and evolve. You might have experienced this already and found that you've grown apart from someone who used to be your best friend. This is a natural part of life, and it happens in adulthood too. It can be difficult, though, if you think the reason for a friendship changing is that there's something wrong with you. So I want to tell you right now that there is nothing wrong with you. Some friendships stick, and some don't. And sometimes when we lose a friend it can change things for the better, because we find new people who allow us to be our most fabulously awesome selves.

But if you are feeling lonely and struggling to connect with others around you, please know that does not mean you will be lonely forever.

> LOTS OF PEOPLE STRUGGLE WITH RELATIONSHIPS IN SCHOOL BUT GO ON TO BUILD AMAZING FRIENDSHIPS LATER ON OR OUTSIDE OF SCHOOL.

Finding people who have a shared interest can be a great way to connect with others. So joining a new club or society based on something you're interested in can be a way to make new friends. It may be scary talking to new people, but remembering that other people are probably just as nervous as you are might help you to feel better.

6 IT'S COOL TO BE KIND

It's official: kindness is good for your health. Kindness can reduce blood pressure and the stress hormone cortisol. It can also boost your mood, self-esteem and compassion. What's more, just *seeing* a kind act may have a positive physical effect, with some research showing it can help to produce the love hormone oxytocin.

Here are some random acts of kindness you could try this week. (I promise the adults in your life did not pay me to write this – these things could genuinely make you feel good, honest!)

HOLD THE DOOR OPEN FOR SOMEONE ELSE.

DO A CHORE WITHOUT BEING ASKED TO DO IT.

WRITE A THANK-YOU NOTE FOR THE PERSON WHO DELIVERS YOUR POST AND STICK IT TO YOUR FRONT DOOR.

DONATE SOME OF YOUR OLD TOYS OR CLOTHES.

TALK TO A NEW PERSON AT SCHOOL.

WRITE A THANK-YOU MESSAGE FOR YOUR TEACHER.

CREATE A DRAWING FOR AN IMPORTANT ADULT IN YOUR LIFE, TELLING THEM HOW MUCH YOU VALUE THEM.

MAKE A GET-WELL CARD FOR A FRIEND OR RELATIVE WHO'S POORLY.

LEND A FRIEND THIS VERY BOOK. (ONCE YOU'VE FINISHED READING IT, OF COURSE!)

When it comes to looking after your body, there is no single way to do it. What feels good for one person might not work for the person next to them. Plus, on some days you may only feel able to manage the most basic acts of self-care, like brushing your teeth or putting on some clean underwear.

THE MOST IMPORTANT THING TO REMEMBER IS THAT YOUR BODY DESERVES RESPECT, AND SO DO YOU.

So how will you celebrate your body today? Hopefully this chapter has given you some ideas for ways to start.

CHAPTER 6

MIRACLE BODY

YOUR BODY HAS BEEN CHANGING FROM THE MOMENT YOU WERE BORN, BECAUSE THIS IS WHAT BODIES DO.

Many of the changes in your body happen so slowly that you probably don't notice them straight away, like your hair or fingernails growing. But other changes, like the ones your body might be going through right now, may feel more noticeable.

During puberty, your body will grow faster than it will at any other time of your life, apart from when you were a baby and toddler. Don't worry, you're not going to suddenly quadruple in size like a *Super Mario* character after collecting a mushroom! But while the changes are slower than those in a computer game, they can still feel confusing. And that is what this chapter is all about: helping you to understand what's going on both inside and on the outside of your miraculous (not-*Super-Mario*) body.

WHAT IS PUBERTY?

Look up the word 'puberty' in a biology textbook and you'll probably get something like:

> THE PRIMARY FUNCTION OF PUBERTY IS TO PRODUCE SEXUALLY MATURE ADULTS CAPABLE OF REPRODUCTION.

Now, you might be thinking, *Errr, sorry? What was that? I'm supposed to be an adult capable of what now?*

We're about to break this definition down in a way that makes sense. Throughout this chapter, we're going to talk about the biological reason for some of the changes that might be happening in your body. However – and this is a BIG however – these biological purposes simply mean a body *can* do something, not that it *has* to, or that it *should*.

So, before we go on, I want to let you know a few really important things to keep in mind while you're reading.

- Just because puberty is about helping a body mature so it can reproduce (as in, make babies), this does not mean that everyone wants babies when they grow up.

- It also does not mean that a person who has gone through puberty has to start thinking about sex.

- Sex is not just about penis-in-vagina sex.

- Sex is one way to make a baby, but there are other ways too.

The other really important thing to say at this point is that going through puberty does not officially make someone an adult. You might feel different from how you did at age five, for example, but the human brain doesn't fully develop until the age of twenty-five. There is more to growing up and becoming an adult than just developing body hair, starting your period or having erections and wet dreams (all of which we'll learn more about in a minute).

Knowing the biological purpose of puberty, though, can help you to understand what's going on in your body, and why it might be happening. This can be a useful tool in supporting your body image as you grow up and experience these physical changes.

PUBERTY AND BODY IMAGE

A key part of positive body image is feeling at home in your body, which can be tricky if it's changing really quickly. This isn't the case for everyone, but for some people a body that was once so comfy simply doesn't feel familiar any more. It's a bit like coming home from school and finding someone's moved all the furniture around in your bedroom.

Puberty can also be a time when other people might make more comments about your appearance than they used to. It's almost as though some people think that, the moment you reach a certain age, your body becomes public property. It can be mega annoying. This might show up as adults going on about how much you've grown (major eye-roll) or people at school making comments about your body or your appearance. You might even find people treat you more like an adult as your body changes. This sounds great on the surface (later bedtimes, yay!), but it might not be so great if it means people start acting like you're much older than you are (*why has Aunty Wendy given me a pair of leopard-print pants for Christmas instead of the usual festive onesie?!*). All this might mean the expectations, pressures and responsibilities heaped on you are too much to cope with. Grown-ups can forget that,

JUST BECAUSE YOUR BODY IS CHANGING, IT DOESN'T MEAN YOU'RE AN ADULT YET.

ADULTIFICATION BIAS

Adultification bias is where people believe some children are more grown up than they are, so they aren't seen as innocent in the same way as other kids their age. Sometimes adultification bias can mean these children are seen as aggressive or more independent, which can result in them being treated unfairly, with higher expectations and harsher punishments, and given more responsibility and less protection than other children.

Researchers have found that adultification bias affects Black children more than white children. It can also affect children whose bodies are bigger than their thin peers, or whose bodies change shape due to puberty earlier.

ADULTIFICATION BIAS IS ANOTHER EXAMPLE OF HOW WE NEED **SOCIETY** TO CHANGE, **NOT OUR BODIES**.

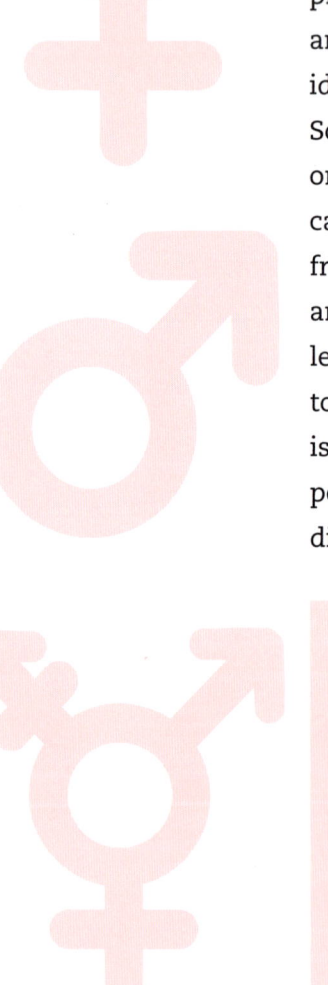

The changes that happen to your body during puberty can also be confusing if you're questioning your gender identity. It may be that the physical changes trigger thoughts and feelings about your gender identity that haven't come up before. Sometimes, for people who are trans or gender non-conforming, puberty can cause feelings of disconnection from the body. This can be confusing and upsetting, and sometimes may lead to mental-health issues related to poor body image. However, this is not always the case, and different people will experience puberty in different ways.

If you're struggling with some of these feelings, it's important to seek support and not try to deal with it alone. This starts with finding a trusted adult to talk to.

Although it might feel like it sometimes, puberty doesn't happen overnight. It's a process, and it usually lasts from around two to five years. Because all bodies are different, there's no set rule for when puberty begins. This means you might notice your best friend starts to go through puberty before you, or vice versa.

The changes your body experiences will be different depending on your sex. This means that, if you were assigned female at birth and have ovaries (the parts of the body next to the womb which produce and release eggs), then the changes happening in your body can start anywhere between the ages of eight and thirteen. If you were assigned male at birth and have testes (the parts of the body that produce sperm), then you're likely to start going through puberty any time between the ages of nine and fifteen.

SO, HERE'S THE SCIENCE . . .

- Puberty begins when your brain releases a special chemical called gonadotropin-releasing hormone, or GnRH for short. (Try saying that quickly!)

- The GnRH makes its way to the pituitary gland, which then releases another two hormones with equally tongue-twisting names: luteinizing hormone (aka LH) and follicle-stimulating hormone (aka FSH). Your body is basically a big hormone party at this point.

- These hormones travel through the blood and get to work triggering changes in your body.

- If you have **ovaries**, the FSH and LH hormones will stimulate them to release yet another hormone called **oestrogen**. If you have **testes**, the FSH and LH hormones will stimulate them to release a hormone called **testosterone**.

- Oestrogen and testosterone are the two hormones that are responsible for most of the physical changes that come with puberty. Their purpose is to make your body mature, so it is capable of reproduction (making a baby) at some point in the future.

A guy called **Professor James M. Tanner** was the first person to identify the stages of physical development that happen in puberty. Thanks to him, these stages are now known as the Tanner Stages (nothing to do with sunbathing). There are five stages in total, and it takes anywhere from two to five years to go through them.

You won't necessarily notice when puberty first starts happening to you. This is because the first stage, in which the brain starts releasing hormones, doesn't result in physical changes straight away.

BODY CHANGES DURING PUBERTY

Once we get to the second stage of puberty, the physical changes start happening. There is a whole range of ways you might notice the visible stages of puberty in your own body and in the bodies of those around you who are a similar age.

BODY HAIR

One of the first physical changes you might notice is the arrival of body hair. It's not like you'll go to sleep one night and wake up the next morning looking like Chewbacca, but it can still feel like a sudden change, particularly if you've never noticed the hair much on your body before. But – news flash! – you have always had hair on your body.

BODY FACT:
The number of hairs on human beings is not that much smaller than the number of hairs on apes – we have about sixty hairs per square centimetre of naked skin.

Millions of years ago, back in the sabre-toothed tiger days, our ancestors would have been covered in thick hair. Over time, we evolved to lose much of this thick hair due to warmer temperatures. Some scientists think this was a way for us to adapt to living in warmer environments, along with developing sweat glands so we could lose heat through sweat. But, while we lost the thick hair all over our bodies, we kept it in certain places – and we kept fine hair everywhere else too. In fact, the only parts of our bodies that *don't* have hair are the soles of our feet, the inside of our wrists, our palms and our lips.

The soft, fine hair that has covered your body since you were a baby is called vellus hair. When you go through puberty some of your vellus hair follicles will become terminal hair follicles, which means the hair that used to be fine will be thicker. This thicker hair only covers certain parts of the body, usually on your pubic area and around your genitals (aka pubic hair, or pubes) and under your armpits. You might also notice hair on other parts of your body that you didn't notice before, like on your legs, arms and face.

This hair has a purpose. Just as your eyelashes protect your eyes and the hairs inside your nostrils protect your nose, the hairs on other parts of your body are there to protect you. Scientists think underarm hair and pubic hair has a purpose too – it's all about sexual selection (which is the scientific way of explaining how people end up fancying each other). Both the underarms and the pubic area have scent-releasing organs called apocrine glands, which are unique to everyone. The hair in these areas helps to trap and disperse the scent, a bit like your very own built-in human air freshener – except the purpose of this air freshener is to get your crush to fancy you, not to hide the stinky smells in the bathroom.

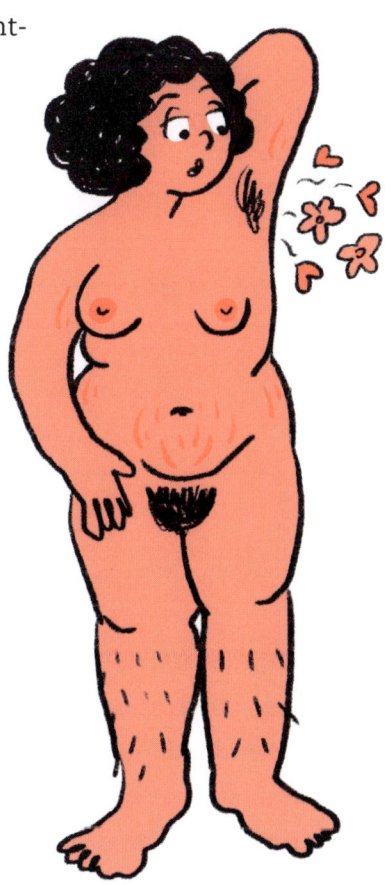

Because body hair often grows in areas of the body that have scent-producing glands, some people believe body hair is unhygienic, but this is totally untrue. Getting rid of the hair in these places won't stop the scent being produced, and anyway it's natural to have body odour.

GOOD HYGIENE MEANS WASHING YOUR BODY, NOT SHAVING YOUR BODY HAIR.

In fact, the practice of removing hair is a **social norm**, another unwritten rule that many people follow and is just considered 'normal' (even if it isn't). Underarm-hair removal started in the early 1900s, when women began wearing sleeveless dresses. Advertisers told women their underarm hair was ugly in a bid to get them to buy razors. They made people feel bad about their bodies as a way to make money, which, as we've already learned, the modern cosmetics industry is still doing over a hundred years later.

IF SOMEONE CHOOSES TO SHAVE THEIR BODY HAIR, THAT IS THEIR CHOICE. BUT IT IS A CHOICE BASED ON BEAUTY STANDARDS, SOCIAL NORMS OR THAT PERSON'S OWN PERSONAL BODY PREFERENCES – NOT HYGIENE.

In response to these beauty standards, many people today are resisting the pressure to remove their body hair. Instead, they proudly show off their beautifully bushy underarms, legs and facial hair. In fact, this trend is now so widespread that some razor companies have switched their messaging to celebrating body hair instead of shaming it.

Harnaam Kaur is a motivational speaker, world-record holder and activist from England. As a teenager, Harnaam was bullied for her facial hair, which was one of the symptoms she experienced as a result of having polycystic ovary syndrome. At the age of sixteen, she decided to stop trying to remove her facial hair and instead embraced it. Harnaam now shares her message of self-love and acceptance through education and public speaking, and has been featured in newspapers and magazines all over the world.

Young children are not brought up knowing what a body should or should not look like, or where hair should or should not be. As we grow older, we conform to society and the beauty standards that are set. We are then labelled, moulded and shaped, and put into boxes, and we become people that we authentically are not.

Harnaam Kaur

BODY SHAPE

Your body will likely change shape quite a bit during puberty. In fact, it's very normal for your body to grow outwards before it grows upwards, because your body stores fat in preparation for growth spurts. Depending on your sex, the fat is likely to be stored in different places on your body. If you have a vulva and a uterus (also called a womb), then fat is more likely to be stored on your hips, thighs and buttocks. If you have testes and a penis, it's more likely to be stored on your stomach.

WEIGHT GAIN IS A TOTALLY NORMAL PART OF PUBERTY.

A side effect of all this growing is that you might also find your appetite increases and you feel hungrier than usual. This is because your body is likely to need more energy than before, as all sorts of things are happening behind the scenes to make your body grow and change.

AN INCREASED APPETITE IS ALSO A TOTALLY NORMAL PART OF PUBERTY.

Another body-shape change you might notice is that you may start to grow breasts. This will happen if you have a uterus, as your ovaries release the hormone oestrogen around your body. Your breasts won't grow into a rounded shape overnight. At first, buds will appear, and the nipple and breast area around the nipple will become slightly raised. The dark area around the nipple, called your areola, may also get a bit bigger.

One of the reasons bodies grow breasts is to produce milk to feed a baby. When a person has a baby, their body will release a hormone that helps the body to make and store milk in little pockets and tubes inside the breast called ducts and lobes. This milk then comes out through the nipples. (Not everyone who has a baby can or wants to breast or chest feed, though.)

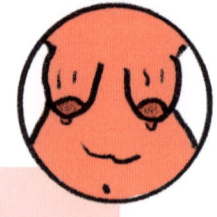

You might think that breasts are all perfectly symmetrical – particularly if the only ones you've seen are in photos of people who have been airbrushed or who have had cosmetic surgery. Breasts look very different on different people, and it's really normal for them to not be a perfectly matching pair, in just the same way it's normal for one of your feet to be slightly bigger than the other.

There's no single timeline for breasts to grow, and you may find they don't become fully developed until you reach the age of seventeen, or even later. Some people may also only grow one breast and find the other never grows. It's totally normal not to develop breasts until you're a bit older, but I used to worry about this a lot when I was at school – which wasn't helped by some of the boys in my class teasing me and calling me flat-chested. If you've noticed anyone at your school making jokes about someone's bra size, it's important to know this isn't OK, and that the problem is with the culture that normalizes these kinds of comments.

YOUR BODY

AND

YOUR BOOBS

ARE

YOUR BUSINESS, AND NO ONE ELSE'S.

If you have a penis and testicles, you may notice that these get bigger during puberty. It's not unusual for the testicles and scrotal sac (or 'balls') to almost double in size during this time, while the penis grows in length first, then width. Just like breasts, testicles are often not the same shape or size, and sometimes one may not grow at all (such as if your testes didn't descend as a baby). Many teenagers worry about the size of their penis, but it's important to know that the size of someone's penis doesn't tell you anything about how 'manly' or 'good at sex' they are, despite what some people might say in the PE changing rooms. What's more, a flaccid (soft) penis doesn't necessarily tell you anything about its size when it's erect. Despite what you may hear from your mates (or the penis doodles you might suddenly start noticing EVERYWHERE in school – what is that about?!),

SIZE DOESN'T MATTER.

If you're feeling self-conscious or worried about your changing body shape, developing breasts or growing penis, then it might help to remember that bodies come in all sorts of shapes and sizes, and there is no single 'right' way to have a body. What's more, no one EVER has the right to comment on or judge your body.

YOUR BODY IS A MIRACLE, AND IT BELONGS TO YOU, NO ONE ELSE.

And finally, if you have any concerns at all about how your body is developing – whether it's your breasts, balls or anything in between, then it's important to speak to a trusted adult. It may be that the thing you're worried about is totally normal, but it's always worth getting advice if you're not 100% sure. It might feel embarrassing to talk about, but remember – all the adults in your life went through puberty themselves too!

BODY CHANGES AND GENDER IDENTITY

The development of breasts or a growing penis can be a confusing time for some children and young people, but particularly for those who are trans, non-binary or gender non-conforming and who feel the body changes they're experiencing don't fit with their gender identity.

If this is you, it's important to speak to a trusted adult about your feelings. There are certain gender-affirming clothes and garments which may help you to feel more comfortable in your body, but it's really important you have the support of an adult to find the right things. This is because using the wrong type of garment (or one that doesn't fit properly) can cause serious discomfort and even affect your health.

Of course, there is no one-size-fits-all way for bodies to be, and not all children who are trans, non-binary or gender non-conforming will feel confused about their changing body, or require special garments to make them feel comfortable.

SKIN CHANGES

You might have noticed your skin starting to change. This is another very normal and natural side effect of puberty, and is due to all those hormonal changes your body is going through. The hormones stimulate the oil glands in your skin, which can provide the perfect conditions for spots to develop, as the tiny hair follicles all over your body (also known as pores) become blocked.

BODY FACT:
The skin is the body's largest organ.

Your skin's job is to provide a protective barrier for your body, keeping your internal organs and skeleton safe. It also allows you to feel things and detect temperatures. Your skin is working really hard for you, even though it might seem like it's just sitting around not doing much. So, although you might feel pressure to have Instagram-perfect skin all the time, it's important to remember that your skin is a living, changing thing and it's totally natural for it to look different day to day. Plus, Instagram-perfect skin isn't real anyway – especially if it's been photographed with a filter. More on that later!

BODY-MYTH ALERT: You only get spots if you don't wash your face enough.

Spots don't just happen during puberty, and they aren't happening because your skin is dirty or you're not washing enough. In fact, sometimes washing *too much* can cause your body to produce extra oil, which can actually mean more spots.

Acne is a common skin condition that inflames the skin and leads to lots of spots developing. Just like body size, acne is partly determined by your genes. It can also be triggered by periods, and the rise in testosterone during puberty. If you have spots that are causing you discomfort, then speak to a trusted adult and ask them to take you to see a doctor, as there are treatments and medications that can help to ease the pain of severe acne.

But also, please know that spots are a very normal part of being human, and that everyone will experience skin changes throughout their lives. Whether you've experienced spots or are yet to have your first pimple, we are all surrounded by images on social media, in advertising and in mainstream media that show flawless skin, which can affect how we feel about our own skin. That old frenemy the beauty industry is very good at convincing us that we need to 'solve' our skin 'problems' in one way or another – usually by using their products.

This kind of attitude can also show up at school, where you may have noticed people making mean comments about others' skin. If you're struggling with this yourself, then please know that you're not alone. I also experienced mean comments about spots on my skin when I was going through puberty and, believe me, I know how much it sucks. But also, know that it's not something you simply have to put up with.

There are many people fighting back against appearance ideals that make us feel bad about our skin. Skin-positivity activists and even many models and actors are arguing that photo editing and filters mean we often don't see what normal, natural skin looks like, spots and all. (We'll talk about this more in the next chapter.)

Constanza Concha is a skin-positivity influencer from Venezuela. She has a rare form of acne called acne conglobata, which causes nodules and abscesses, and which she developed around the age of nine years old. She now has tens of thousands of followers on Instagram who are inspired by the very real, untouched photos she posts and her message of skin positivity.

I think that beauty comes from within. If I am at peace with the person that I am, then no one else's perception of me should matter.

Constanza Concha

MENSTRUATION

Periods happen because – surprise, surprise – those hormones in the body are having a party again. In the case of periods, it's the hormones oestrogen and progesterone, which cause the lining of the uterus to build up. This is happening in preparation for reproduction – the womb lining thickens so that a fertilized egg can attach itself there and develop into a foetus.

BODY FACT:
Every month, 1.8 billion people around the world have a period.

Even if the body you have means you'll never experience a period, knowing how and why they happen is still important, so please don't skip ahead to the next bit! Menstrual justice, period positivity and period poverty are all things everyone should know about, whether they menstruate or not. (More on all this soon.)

Anyway, back to the biology lesson. If there's no fertilized egg, then the lining of the uterus breaks down and bleeds away, which results in a period. On average, it takes around a month for the lining to build back up again, which is why periods generally happen around once a month.

Before your periods start, you might notice something called vaginal discharge in your knickers or pants. This substance is thin, clear or whitish in colour, and is produced by the increased oestrogen levels in your body. Like many aspects of puberty, this discharge has a function, which is to prevent infection in the vagina and keep it moisturized and healthy.

THE VAGINA IS LITERALLY A SELF-CLEANING MIRACLE.

You can expect your period to begin around a year after getting this white discharge, or two years after the first signs of puberty. All bodies are unique, and there's not a single timeline every body follows, but generally the arrival of your period could happen anywhere from the age of ten to sixteen.

When your period begins, you'll see a reddish-brown stain in your pants or on your bed sheets. Don't worry, blood won't suddenly start spurting everywhere like something from a horror film. It's actually a lot less blood than most people think.

BODY FACT:

Around one to five tablespoons of blood is lost during one period (even though it might look like a lot more).

You'll need to use sanitary products to absorb or collect the blood, so it doesn't leak out of your underwear on to your clothes. When someone first starts having a period, it's unlikely it'll be super regular for the first few years. It's also unlikely their period will stick around for the same number of days every time. This can be annoying and unpredictable, which is why it's useful to always be prepared, just in case (more on that in a minute). Once things settle down and periods become more regular, they usually last two to seven days, and happen every twenty-eight days, or between twenty-three and thirty-five days.

The blood loss from a period itself doesn't hurt, but it's not unusual to experience cramps in your tummy or back.

Many people call these period pains, and they can make some of us (including me) feel quite unwell. If you're suffering with this, then you might find it comforting to use a heat pad or hot-water bottle, or to have a bath.

YOUR BODY KNOWS WHAT IT NEEDS – YOU JUST HAVE TO SLOW DOWN AND LISTEN TO IT.

You may need to rest more, or to pause some of the more physically demanding activities you do every day. If your period pains are causing you some serious discomfort, then it's also important to speak to a trusted adult as severe pain can sometimes be a sign of an underlying condition that needs treatment.

If you don't get periods but know someone who does, be gentle with them if you know they're having their period.

The hormones and body processes happening during a period can cause mood swings and intense emotions, along with feelings of tiredness. You don't need to fetch them snacks or hot-water bottles (although that is always welcome). Just being kind and not expecting them to function at full speed goes a long way.

BODY-MYTH ALERT: Periods are dirty.

Historically, periods have often been a taboo subject, and some people have seen them as something to be ashamed of. (Taboo means something that is seen as unacceptable and not to be spoken about.) For a long time, people believed that only cisgender women could have periods, when actually trans people, non-binary people, intersex people and gender non-conforming people can have periods too. People also used to believe that the role of cisgender women was to be 'pure'. So the idea of periods as 'dirty' comes from another body ideal that says women should be clean and pure, and which discriminates against all people who menstruate.

In fact, when sanitary pads first went on sale in the United States in 1896, they didn't sell very well because many women and menstruating people were too embarrassed to buy them. They preferred to use the rags and cotton for babies' nappies than admit publicly they had their period. By the 1920s, there were more period products on offer, but people were still too embarrassed to buy them and didn't want to ask for them out loud. Shop owners got round this by placing secret boxes on the counter that someone could put their money in before being given a discreetly wrapped package with their goods.

Nowadays period products can be found on supermarket shelves rather than hidden in boxes, but there is still a lack of openness surrounding periods. People who don't have periods are often not educated about them, and those who do have periods may try to hide them (for example, by stashing a tampon up their sleeve when they have to go to the loo to change it). This silence is also damaging to people who menstruate but don't identify with the gender they were assigned at birth, because they often aren't given the information or support they need.

Kenny Ethan Jones is a writer and activist who made history as the first trans man to front a period campaign.

Every person deserves to be informed on their health in a way that aligns with their gender identity. For me, I felt alienated, like periods shouldn't be part of my lived experience, which made me avoid learning about them. This meant I wasn't equipped to take care of my health, and reinforced that the subject was taboo.

Kenny Ethan Jones

Some of the fear and shame around periods can be traced back thousands of years. In ancient Rome, for example, a man called Pliny the Elder (what a name!) wrote that 'naked menstruating women' were so terrifying they could prevent hailstorms and lightning, and scare insects away from crops. (I mean, I wish this were true – maybe those lettuces in my veg patch would have survived if so.) But in other ancient cultures, periods were often seen as a sign of power, life, vitality and even magic. The ancient Mayans believed period blood contained a special spiritual energy, and in ancient Egypt some people thought it could be used in certain medicines.

Today, many people are trying to smash the taboos around periods.

THE PERIOD POSITIVITY MOVEMENT IS A SOCIAL-JUSTICE MOVEMENT PUSHING FOR GREATER OPENNESS AROUND PERIODS AND MENSTRUATION KNOWLEDGE.

There are people working hard to tackle period poverty, which is when people can't afford to buy menstrual products. And there are activists working on menstrual justice issues, challenging shame around periods and working to change the law so it's fairer for people who have periods (such as making it illegal to fire or punish someone for taking time off work due to a painful or very heavy period).

HOW TO BE PERIOD-PREPARED

Annoyingly, your period doesn't send you a text message two weeks before its arrival. This means that you could start bleeding when you're not expecting it.

With that in mind, there are a few things you can do to be prepared, so that when it does happen you've got everything you need. One way to do this is to pack a period bag, which is essentially a little pouch or wallet you can put in your school bag with everything you need.

Some things you could put in your period bag include:

- sanitary towels

- a change of pants or knickers

- baby wipes

- a small plastic, compost or cloth bag to store your soiled pants in if you need to change them at school.

There are lots of different types of period products you can get now, including absorbent pants called period pants and many different types of sanitary pads, including reusable ones. There are also products that you can insert inside the vagina to absorb or collect the blood, such as tampons or menstrual cups.

You may find it easier at first to use either sanitary pads, which stick inside your underwear, or absorbent period pants. Then, as you get more used to having your period, you can experiment with different types of products to find out which works best for you.

If you're unsure about which product to use, or how to use it, find a trusted adult to talk to. They can help you work out what's right for you – and maybe you could even look up some of the cool videos and support on period positive websites too. Tampons, particularly, can be tricky to use at first, and they need to be changed regularly or they carry the risk of something called toxic shock syndrome, which can be dangerous.

ERECTIONS

We usually think about erections as something that happens to a penis. This isn't strictly true but, for the purposes of this bit of the book, we're talking about the process that happens when a penis goes hard. If you've got a penis, you might already know an erection can happen at any age, but it's likely to happen more often during puberty, due to all those hormones partying in your body.

Just as with periods, it can help to know *why* erections happen, as this can help you to understand what's going on with your body when your penis goes hard. So here's another mini biology lesson. The penis contains two chambers – a bit like tunnels – which run the length of the penis and contain a whole maze of blood vessels. Each blood vessel is like a mini room inside the penis. An erection is caused by nerve messages stimulating the penis, which cause those rooms (or blood vessels) to relax and open up, allowing the blood to flow in and fill up the space. This makes the penis go hard.

But what sets those nerves off to start sending messages in the first place? Well, there has to be some kind of sensory (touch) or mental (thought) stimulation. It could be that you've touched your penis and it's gone hard, or that you've thought about something that has aroused you, causing the nerves to start sending messages. Often, though, erections can be out of your control, and sometimes you might get one and have no idea where it came from – a bit like when you randomly start hiccupping. Erections can happen at any time, which can be annoying if you're in double maths on a Monday morning or sharing a cup of tea with your gran. Some people find that crossing their legs carefully or putting a bag, cushion or coat in their lap can help in these situations.

Having an erection doesn't mean you're ready to have sex. It's just your body's way of preparing for reproduction. (Again, this doesn't mean you ever have to have a baby, or that sex is only about making babies, or that sex is just about penis-in-vagina sex. Just thought I'd remind you of that, in case you forgot.)

Anyway, the biological purpose of the body being able to have an erection is to help the penis release sperm to fertilize an egg. For adults who choose to have sex, an erection can help them to have penis-in-vagina sex (which is one kind of what is also known as penetrative sex) with another consenting adult. The sperm comes out of the penis and goes into the vagina, and if an egg has been released by the ovaries it may get fertilized by the sperm. This is the start of conception and reproduction.

All this to say that, just because your penis is capable of an erection, it does not mean you ever have to use your penis to have penetrative sex – neither with a person with a vagina nor anyone else. There are lots of different ways to have sex, and lots of different types of sexuality. Ultimately, the most important thing to remember as you grow up is this:

YOUR PENIS,
YOUR RULES.

A person with a vulva can get an erection too – this will be big news for some people! – but because of the shape of the vulva it won't be as noticeable. Let's take a quick tour around the vulva, so I can explain.

- The **vulva** is the outer part of the genitals. It leads to the **vagina**, which is inside the body. The vulva consists of the **labia majora** (the outer skin fold or lips), **the labia minora** (the inner skin fold or lips) and the **clitoris**.

- The clitoris is a bulb-shaped organ around the size of a pea that contains thousands of nerve endings – that's more than anywhere else in the body when you compare areas of the same size.

- It's protected by the **clitoral hood**, which is a fold of skin connected to the labia minora (inner lips) at the front of the vulva.

- The tip of the clitoris is the external clitoris, and it varies in size from person to person.

- This isn't the only part of the clitoris, though. The rest of it is internal, so isn't visible. In total, when you count both the internal and external parts of the clitoris, it can be over twelve centimetres long!

Wow!

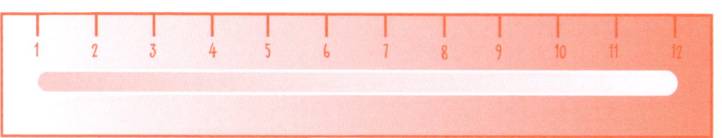

The clitoris is made of similar material to the penis. And, just like the penis, it can swell and go erect. This is called arousal. Just as blood flows to the penis to make it hard when a person is aroused, the same thing happens to the clitoris.

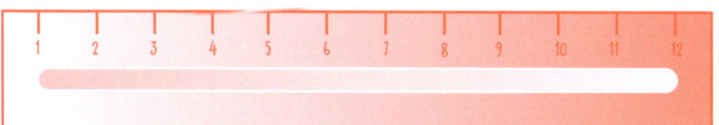

Debbie Bere (aka Sex Debbie) is an educator who works with children and adults to help them learn about sex and relationships.

Arousal is normal and can be caused by all sorts of different things – some expected and some unexpected. You may find it feels good to touch your own body in different ways, but being aware of your environment if or when you do this is important.

Debbie Bere

You don't have to be awake to have an erection. If you have a dream that arouses you, it's totally normal for the penis or clitoris to swell up. And, in some cases, you might have an orgasm, which is where the sexual tension in your body is released. When this happens in your sleep, it's called a wet dream. If you have a penis, it will release something called semen – a white fluid that contains sperm, which fertilizes an egg during reproduction. The process when semen comes out of the penis is known as ejaculation. The semen is often wet and sticky when it is first released, but when it dries it can go crusty and a bit hard. It's really normal to wake up and realize that you've ejaculated in your sleep. This is nothing to worry about or to feel ashamed of. If this happens, you can clean yourself up by having a wash and changing and washing your bedding.

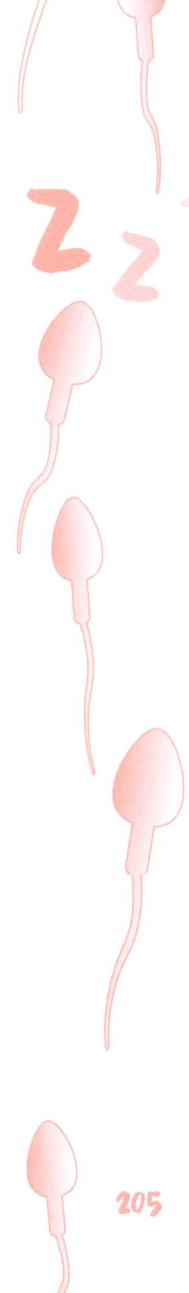

PERSONAL HYGIENE DURING PUBERTY

Keeping your body clean is an important act of self-care, and a way to respect and be kind to your changing, miraculous body. Wash regularly, and make sure you wash your body properly and thoroughly. This means soaping under your arms and all over your body.

When you wash your genitals, take care not to use scented or strong soap, as this can cause irritation. If you have a penis with a foreskin (the fold of skin that covers the tip of some, but not all, penises), make sure you pull the foreskin back to wash thoroughly underneath it.

If you have a vulva, wash it with warm water, spreading the lips apart and cleaning gently in the folds.

Avoid using soap on your vulva or getting soap inside your vagina or down the tip of your penis, as this can cause irritation.

VOICE CHANGES

It's not just the things on the outside of your body that are growing and changing. As you go through puberty, your voice box – which is called the larynx, and lives in your throat – gets bigger and thicker too. The larynx is essentially two muscles, also known as vocal cords, that are a bit like elastic bands that stretch across the throat. When you speak, air from the lungs rushes up to make these muscles vibrate – that's what causes the sound of your voice. As the larynx grows, the sound of your voice will change.

If you have a vulva, your voice will only change by a couple of tones and you may not even notice it. If you have a penis, the change is likely to be more obvious, as your voice will get quite a bit deeper. This can lead to unpredictable squeaky-voice moments, which can sound even higher than Sam Ryder hitting a top note at Eurovision. If this happens to you, know that it's totally normal and nothing to be ashamed of. Try to just go with it, and don't be afraid to laugh. You could even do some air guitar to really style it out!

UNPREDICTABLE EMOTIONS

The final thing we're going to talk about on this wild ride of puberty is the stuff you can't see: your emotions. These changing emotions can feel scary at times, like they come out of nowhere and you have no control over them. Lots of people refer to 'raging' hormones during puberty, which makes me think of frothy waves in an angry ocean, with thunder and lightning flashing overhead. The real thing isn't quite so dramatic, although it may feel that way sometimes.

It doesn't help when adults blame all your big feelings on those hormones rushing around your body. They might say stuff like, 'Oh it's just the hormones,' and roll their eyes. (Thanks for your feedback, Aunty Wendy.) I remember this happening to me, and it made me even angrier, or sadder, or more frustrated. When this happens, it may help to send your brain a clear signal that you're safe and everything is OK, as this can help you to ride out the feeling. You can also use some of the hacks for looking after your mind and body from Chapter 5, and find someone to talk the feelings through with. Maybe not Aunty Wendy, though.

PUBERTY: UNLOCKED!

Phew, that was a whistle-stop tour of your MIRACLE body. Hopefully it's given you some information that may be useful as you navigate the stormy seas of puberty. (That really is a bad metaphor. No need to start saying, 'Arrghh, me hearties!' like you're some kind of puberty pirate.)

But seriously, if you're finding all the changes in your body overwhelming, that's totally normal.

IT'S OK TO BE IN AWE OF YOUR MIRACLE BODY AT THE SAME TIME AS BEING A BIT FRUSTRATED BY IT.

As we learned earlier, you can love something and still be annoyed by it sometimes (like your dog, or your best friend, or, yes, even your parents).

You may feel like you want to bottle these feelings up or distract yourself from everything that's going on inside you. This can seem particularly easy when distraction is in your pocket in the form of a phone. We're going to talk about this in the next chapter, because your phone, social media and the big, glittery world of the internet can both support your body image *and* damage it.

CHAPTER 7

FILTERED BODY

Unless you live in a cave on a hill and have never, ever communicated with the outside world, you'll already be aware of social media. And, if I can hazard a guess, I bet you already know about not speaking to strangers online, not sharing information about yourself, and that social-media platforms have a minimum age limit. (I can see you rolling your eyes from here.) Don't worry, this chapter is not an internet-safety lecture.

But – and this is a BIG but – before we dive into the many aspects of social media and body image, I want you to know that, just because all your mates might be using social media, and just because you've got a phone, and just because your favourite celeb is a social-media influencer, it does not mean that *you* have to use social media yourself at any point, ever.

Loads of people choose not to use social media at all, for very valid reasons. Doing what feels right for you and treading your own path is a really healthy and brilliant thing to do. But even if you have absolutely zero interest in ever using social media, this chapter might still be helpful, because it can help you to understand some of the ways that social media affects how people feel about their bodies, including some of your friends or classmates at school.

INTRODUCING FACE-FILTER CULTURE

You're growing up in a world with the internet in your pocket, where billions of photos are shared online every day, along with more than 720,000 hours of video. You're probably already aware that many of these photos and videos aren't real. They've been edited, photoshopped, cropped and manipulated to look like something they're not. To put it simply: you can't always take someone's online face at face value.

BODY FACT:

More than 3.2 billion images are shared every day online.

Before we had front-facing cameras on phones, it used to be quite hard to take a picture of yourself. In fact, back in the olden days when I was growing up, phones didn't even have cameras. (Mind-blowing, I know!) But now, an average of 450 selfies are taken per person per year, and many of these are uploaded to the internet. It's really common to go to a famous landmark and see people taking photos not of the landmark itself but of themselves standing in front of it. (This happens in art galleries and museums too – no wonder the *Mona Lisa* looks so unimpressed.)

It's not just that we're taking more photos of ourselves. It's that we're seeing more photos of other people too. Even if these photos haven't been put through a filter or edited in some way, they may have been taken using a 'beauty' or 'studio' setting on a camera, which means that often even the most natural-looking photo doesn't actually look how it would in real life. And it doesn't end there. Even online video platforms like Zoom have a 'beauty' setting. So, you could be talking to your best mate or your gran in a video call, and the face you see through the screen is different from what you'd see if you were in the room together.

All this can affect the way you feel about your body. This is because of something called social comparison, which describes the way people learn to value themselves by comparing themselves to others. Even if your appearance is not super important to you and you know that all bodies are good bodies, it's hard not to be affected by the constant stream of images that are edited to make bodies and faces look thinner and smoother and lighter. And, if those images are of your best friends and people you know from school, the impact can be even worse. You probably know you shouldn't compare yourself to a celebrity, but it's harder to avoid the comparison trap with someone you see every day on the school bus.

Social media adds another dimension in the form of pressure from likes, comments and followers. These are a sort of online currency that can make people feel like they're rich, powerful and important if they get a lot of  them. But what happens if you post a selfie and it doesn't get many – or any – likes? If you allow selfies to define your self-worth and compare your own likes to the number your mates get, it might make you  feel like your face or body isn't up to scratch.

THE TRUTH IS,
YOUR WORTH AS A HUMAN
BEING ON THIS PLANET
CAN'T
BE MEASURED BY LIKES,
COMMENTS OR FOLLOWERS —
BUT IT CAN BE HARD TO REMEMBER
THIS WHEN YOU'RE SUCKED
RIGHT INTO THE CENTRE OF THE
SOCIAL-MEDIA VORTEX.

The other impact of face-filter culture is that it can make us want to buy things. Again, that sneaky social comparison steps in to make us feel like we're not as good as someone if we don't have the same stuff as them. But we might also be tricked into believing that, if we just buy that cream, eat that food or get that outfit, we'll look like the filtered face in the photo.

A BODY-HAPPY SHOPPING GUIDE

Here's a handy guide to help you to avoid the effects of face-filter culture and social comparison next time you're out shopping on the high street or online.

BEFORE YOU GO

It's hard (maybe even impossible) to avoid falling for the latest trends. But before you go on your shopping trip or start adding things to your cart, here are three questions you can ask yourself to decide whether or not that latest must-have item is really worth your precious pennies.

1 Do I want it because I think it'll make me look different or be more like someone I've seen online?

2 Have I seen it in sponsored posts online and, if so, had I ever heard of it before then?

3 Will I use it regularly, will it bring me joy and will it add value to my life?

If your answer is yes for question 1, yes then no for question 2, and no for question 3 . . . then maybe it's not something to add to your shopping list.

DO YOUR RESEARCH

Although many shops have got better at creating clothes in a wide range of sizes, there are still some that have work to do! If you're worried about finding clothes that fit comfortably, it can help to do some research to find out which brands are size-inclusive. This is also useful if you're shopping for clothes on pre-loved websites or apps, because you can search by the name of the brand.

DO THE EYES-SHUT TEST

Wearing clothes that don't fit properly can be bad for your body image, because they make you think about your body more than you need to. This can mean you focus on how your body looks in the moment, rather than enjoying the moment itself. If you are a sighted person, you can do this quick test to avoid choosing an outfit based solely on what it looks like on your body:

> BEFORE YOU EVEN LOOK AT YOURSELF IN THE MIRROR, **CLOSE YOUR EYES AND FOCUS ON WHAT THE CLOTHES FEEL LIKE ON YOUR BODY.**

Can you easily bend, reach up high and move around without the clothes rubbing or pinching? If the answer is yes, you may have found your new best (clothes) friend. Or you could go even further and choose a whole range of clothes in a whole range of sizes and then try them all on with your eyes shut. Bonus points if you pull some dance moves at the same time.

Given everything I've just shared about face-filter culture and social comparison, you might assume all social media makes everyone feel bad about their body. Wrong! The truth is, like most things in life, it's complicated and (annoyingly) two things can be true at the same time.

Yes, social media can lead to social comparison and ramp up appearance pressures. But social media has also acted like a megaphone for things like the body positivity movement and the work of fat activists. It can be a tool for celebrating body diversity, and a place to see a wider range of bodies than you might on TV or in films. This is called representation, and it's good news for your body image.

WHEN PEOPLE SEE **THEMSELVES** REPRESENTED IN ANY FORM OF MEDIA, IT CAN **HELP THEM TO** FEEL **RECOGNIZED, AND TO** ACCEPT AND CELEBRATE THEIR DIFFERENCES.

Kim Chi is a digital creator, make-up brand owner, author and the first Korean-American drag queen to appear on *RuPaul's Drag Race*, a reality TV show where drag queens compete for the crown of Drag Superstar.

Looking back now, all the things I hated about myself are all the things that made me special. I just wish I could've realized it back then. It also made me aware of how important diversity and representation is for our future generation.

Kim Chi

MAKING SOCIAL MEDIA WORK FOR YOU

The trick to having a healthy relationship with social media lies in how you use it. This is because of something called algorithms, which are basically the engines driving social-media platforms. Just like computers, the human brain also uses algorithms to work, because an algorithm is simply a set of instructions that help us to come to a decision. In social media, the algorithm is basically an equation which helps a platform to work out what content to show in your feed.

The more you look at a certain type of content, the more that type of content will be offered to you. This means that, if you regularly look up content featuring the filtered faces of celebrities offering beauty and diet hacks, then this is the type of content you will most regularly see on social media. Whereas if you follow people challenging some of these ideas in the form of anti-diet and body-positive content that celebrates all bodies, then that's the type of content you will most likely be shown.

One impact of algorithms – and a criticism of social media itself – is that they can cause **confirmation bias**. This is when we look at information and make decisions based on ideas that match the beliefs and values we already have. Another term for this is an 'echo chamber', where people only talk to or follow people online who agree with all the things they already think. While listening to people you agree with might be comforting and a way of building community, it can also mean that you don't end up thinking for yourself, or that you are never exposed to ideas that might challenge you or encourage you to think about things from another perspective.

For this reason, I often deliberately look up the work of people online who I know I'm likely to disagree with. I'm interested to know what they think, so that I can try to understand their point of view, even if I don't agree with it. I also remind myself that, even if I choose to follow someone online, it doesn't mean I have to agree with every single thing they say or do. Maybe I just really like the photos they share of their dog.

Another way to avoid falling into the echo-chamber trap is to make sure you're following a wide range of accounts. If you decide to start using social media (once you're old enough to use it), be sure to follow all sorts of accounts about all sorts of things you're interested in. Don't just stick to beauty influencers or sports stars. There are accounts about so many different things! (My personal favourites on Instagram are about books and cushions . . . maybe not the most exciting content but, as you know, I was born a thousand years ago.)

FOLLOWING ALL KINDS OF ACCOUNTS WILL KEEP YOUR FEED INTERESTING AND MEAN YOU'RE LESS LIKELY TO BE EXPOSED TO HARMFUL CONTENT THAT MIGHT MAKE YOU FEEL BAD ABOUT YOUR BODY.

Just like you clear out your old clothes from time to time, it can help to have a clear-out (aka an unfollow session) of your social media account too! This is a useful thing to do regularly with a trusted adult who may be able to help you spot if some of those accounts who've snuck into your feed are actually posting harmful content disguised as funny, cool or inspirational. Things aren't always what they seem on social media and it's not always easy to spot the dodgy stuff.

225

Researchers have found that viewing body-positive content online can make people feel better about their own bodies. There's also evidence to show that unfollowing, muting or blocking accounts that promote body ideals and diet culture can be good for body image too. If your feed is only full of bodies, though, you might then fall into the trap of thinking that someone's body – whatever it looks like – is the most important thing about them. So, along with a diverse range of bodies in your feed, make sure you're following a diverse range of accounts full stop.

TROLLING

Trolling is the act of deliberately seeking out arguments and conflict online. Unfortunately, many social-media accounts thrive on conflict, because the more comments a post has – even if those comments are arguing against the original post – the more attention it is likely to get. This means that people will often post content deliberately designed to cause conflict, in the hope it will bring the post more engagement.

Some people will even post body-shaming content that they know will upset people in order to get a reaction, or they might write nasty comments about someone's body underneath that person's post. Health-concern trolling is where a person pretends they are innocently asking a question – such as, 'But what about this person's health?' – as a way to disguise body-shaming someone online.

If you ever encounter trolling online, the best thing to do is to tell a trusted adult straight away, then block and report the account that made the comment.

SOCIAL MEDIA AND MENTAL HEALTH

Even if you're using social media as a tool to boost your body image, being online a lot can still have a negative effect on your mental health, and it can even affect your ability to form meaningful friendships offline. The problem is that social-media platforms have been designed to keep us online as long as possible. They make money by selling ad space to brands, and the more people who use a social-media platform, and the longer they use it for, the more views those ads get.

Social-media companies know that in order to make more money they need to keep people online for longer, and they use lots of clever techniques to do this. Notifications, suggested content, algorithms based on your interests and likes, short videos and trending songs . . . all of these are techniques to try to stop you from putting your phone down.

Simply knowing this isn't always enough to avoid falling into the trap. That's why setting a boundary for yourself, or following the boundary the adults in your life suggest, is important. This might mean:

AGREEING TO TURN YOUR PHONE OFF
AT A SPECIFIC TIME EACH EVENING

NOT TAKING YOUR PHONE
INTO YOUR BEDROOM

NOT HAVING YOUR PHONE
AT THE DINNER TABLE

MAKING SURE YOU HAVE REGULAR
SOCIAL-MEDIA BLACKOUT DAYS, WHERE
YOU DON'T GO ONLINE AT ALL.

I know this probably all sounds really boring, but remember, these sites have been designed to keep you hooked. Making a conscious decision to switch off is an empowering and rebellious act.

SMART SOCIAL-MEDIA TIPS

1. Take regular breaks or blackout days.

2. Follow a diverse range of accounts about lots of different interests and subjects.

3. Do a regular check-up on your feed to ensure you're following a wide range of people with diverse body types.

4. Unfollow or mute accounts that promote idealized bodies, good versus bad bodies, dieting or appearance ideals.

5. Tell a trusted adult if you ever experience or witness trolling online, then block and report the troll.

6 Get out of your echo chamber occasionally. Looking up the opinions of someone you disagree with doesn't mean you have to follow them, but it will open your mind to other perspectives. Remember, you don't have to agree with someone to try to learn more about their point of view.

7 Don't assume that, just because someone has millions of followers online, they are an expert. And never idolize someone just because they have lots of followers. Even your favourite social-media influencer is a human who, just like you, is capable of messing up and making mistakes.

8 Remember that things aren't always as they seem on social media. Even the most harmless-looking content can sometimes carry a harmful message. Speak to your trusted adults and do regular check-ups together on who you're following.

I get it. Growing up is tough enough without worrying about finding a perfectly healthy relationship with social media. And, to be honest, I'm not even sure perfect exists anyway (unless we're talking about the perfect chocolate brownie, in which case it has to be gooey in the middle, and if you disagree you clearly don't know about chocolate brownies).

Maybe you'll decide not to use social media at all, and that is totally OK. Maybe you'll fall down a scrolling spiral of doom occasionally, in which case welcome to the club, because me too! Remember, it's not your fault if this happens. The platforms are literally designed to keep you plugged in.

As we've already covered, social media can be both bad and good. One of the brilliant things about it is that it allows you to explore your identity at an age when you're figuring out what your passions are.

REMEMBER, THOUGH, THAT SOCIAL MEDIA IS ALSO A REALLY PUBLIC WAY TO WORK OUT WHO YOU ARE.

Posting something on social media might feel like a private thing – just between you and your phone – but if your account is public then literally anyone (including Aunty Wendy or your maths teacher) can see it. That's not to say that, once you're old enough, you shouldn't pursue your dream of being the next Kim Chi or Flamingo (if you know, you know). But it's something to keep in mind if you do decide to dip your toe into the social-media vortex.

The key to all of this is that golden word,

'BOUNDARIES'.

Boundaries aren't just about how much you use social media or what you post. They're also about how you talk and think about the bodies you see while you're using social media. And they're about how you navigate comments that might come up about your own body. Which is what we're going to talk about in the next chapter . . .

CHAPTER 8

NOT YOUR BODY

You are human and I am human, but the ways we each experience the world, our relationship with our body and our life up to this moment are probably very different. I want to remind you of this, because it's really common to assume that, just because you feel a certain way or have had a certain experience, everyone else will be the same.

Our differences are what make us human, but sometimes people can forget that we are all different and that, actually, we don't all like the same things. These preferences go beyond simply what flavour of ice cream you choose on a hot sunny day (mint choc chip – don't judge me). They also include how you think and feel about your body, and what you're comfortable with when it comes to your body.

THIS IS WHAT THIS CHAPTER IS ABOUT:

THE FACT THAT **YOUR** BODY IS NOT **MY** BODY, OR **ANYONE ELSE'S** BODY.

WE NEED TO RESPECT THIS ABOUT ONE ANOTHER.

WHAT ARE BOUNDARIES?

Boundaries exist everywhere, but we can't always see them. If you think about your school playground, for example, the fence that goes around it is visible and solid. That fence is a boundary that tells you where you can play and where you're allowed to be. Unlike that fence, body boundaries are invisible, but they're no less important.

The problem is, not everyone's body boundaries look the same. Some people are cool with hugging or being hugged, for example, while others might absolutely hate it. And, sometimes, people aren't really aware of or don't respect body boundaries, which means they can try to pull your body-boundary fence down or tread all over it. Like when Aunty Wendy tries to force you to give her a hug despite the fact you don't want to.

BOUNDARIES AND BODY IMAGE

Body boundaries aren't just about avoiding hugs or kisses from your relatives. They're also about the ways we talk about other people's bodies, and the ways we feel about these types of comments on our own body.

If people are constantly commenting on your body, it might be harder to feel comfortable in your body and to appreciate what it does for you – which is a crucial part of positive body image. These types of comments might also make you feel like your body doesn't really belong to you, especially if the comments come from people close to you who act like your body is their business. And the less you feel like your body is your own, the less connected to and at home in it you may feel.

These comments about bodies can happen both on and offline. For example, you might post a photo of yourself on holiday and find lots of people comment not on what you're doing in the photo but on what you look like. This might make you think about your appearance when it never really crossed your mind before – you just wanted to show off that amazing sandcastle you made with your little brother.

The way other people treat your body may also lead you to think your body is the problem, instead of their behaviour towards it. If you are bullied for the way you look, for example, you may blame your own body (instead of the bullies) and think that the solution is to try to change your appearance. Again, this can happen both in real life and online.

This is why boundaries are a really important aspect of looking after your own body image and creating a world where all bodies are valued. Boundaries are like a cross between a big wall and a giant piece of bubble wrap round your body image. They help to protect your body image, so that you can feel happy in your body, while also reminding you what is and isn't acceptable when it comes to the way you treat other people's bodies.

BODY FACT:
Touch messages are carried around your body at 200 miles per hour.

YOUR TOUCH SYSTEM

Neuroscientists have found there are different types of touch, and they form your body's touch system.

- Discriminative touch is how you feel pressure and vibration. This part of your touch system tells you detailed information about what you've touched and where you've been touched.

- Affective touch is the way humans sometimes convey social and emotional information, like through a hug, pat or stroke on the arm.

There is some evidence that the way we experience these types of touch, and what we feel comfortable with, might vary depending on whether we are neurodivergent or **neurotypical**. For someone who is neurodivergent, for example, a stroke on the arm or a hug may feel extremely uncomfortable. There are lots of reasons a person may not like affective touch, and it is never their job to justify it. It's enough for them to simply say, 'I don't like hugs,' and leave it at that.

And for those who do like hugs, it's really important to ask before hugging someone else. If they don't want to be hugged, you then need to accept that not everyone is the same as you and that other people's body boundaries must be respected. (PS Pass this on to Aunty Wendy.)

Your body is your own, and only you get to have an opinion on it. You're also in charge of how it's treated and what you do with it. This isn't always easy to remember, particularly if you have to follow rules that affect your body, like wearing a school uniform or going to bed at a time set by your parents or caregivers.

These rules don't mean that your body is not your own, though, and mustn't be confused with moments when adults or friends overstep a body boundary and don't respect how you want your body to be treated or talked about. You have every right to say no in these situations. Your body, your rules.

HOW TO BUILD HEALTHY BODY BOUNDARIES

OK, so here's the thing. Your body boundaries are not *just* your business (even though your body is). No matter how good you might be at setting your own boundaries, it can be hard to stick to them if they're being ignored by other people. So if you're finding body boundaries hard, give yourself a break and know that you're not alone and it's not your fault. There are loads of adults who struggle with this stuff too.

To help you find a good place to start, let's look at some ways you can build healthy body boundaries. Strengthening your boundaries is not a race, and you don't get a certificate at the end.

BODY BOUNDARIES THIS WAY

IT'S A MARATHON, NOT A SPRINT . . .

They're something you just need to keep working at slowly over time. (FYI, I'm a fully grown adult and this stuff is literally my job, but I still need to remind myself of these things!)

BUILD YOUR EMPATHY MUSCLES

Empathy is your ability to understand and think about the feelings of another person. There's science to show that empathy isn't just something we learn as we grow up, but also something that we inherit within our genes. So the ability to understand other perspectives and take other people's feelings into consideration is something that some people will find easier than others, depending on their genes, how their brain works, how they've been raised and their own life experiences.

Empathy is an important part of body boundaries, because thinking about the feelings of another person will help you to consider and respect how they want their body to be treated. Being empathetic isn't just about how you treat other people, though. It's also about how you treat yourself.

BUILDING YOUR
EMPATHY MUSCLES
WILL HELP YOU TO BE
KIND TO OTHER PEOPLE
AND
TO YOURSELF.

(I'm calling them muscles, but these aren't physical muscles – they're mental ones. You don't need massive biceps to be empathetic!)

Empathy is something that can be learned and practised, just like playing the guitar, juggling or any other brilliant new skill. One way to build your empathy muscles is to be curious and have conversations with people. Rather than using the time when another person is talking to think about what you want to say, try to really listen to them without interrupting. Try to understand their point of view. The more you learn about all sorts of people, either from conversations in real life or from reading books or watching TV, the more you'll be able to consider things from their perspective.

② PRACTISE BODY RESPECT

At this point, we've covered lots of ways to practise body respect, both in the way you look after your body and in the way you talk to yourself about your body.

POSITIVE AFFIRMATIONS, DAILY SELF-CARE, DEVELOPING HEALTHY HABITS AND TALKING TO YOURSELF LIKE YOU WOULD TO YOUR BEST FRIEND ARE ALL WAYS TO PRACTISE BODY RESPECT.

Body respect doesn't end with how you think and feel about your own body, though. Remember everything we learned about body diversity and recognizing your own body privilege? Body respect is both about how you treat your own body *and* how you treat others' bodies too. In order to really understand body respect, we all need to recognize our own body privilege and be aware that other people will face different pressures on their bodies that might not be the same as our own experiences.

❸ LEARN TO SAY NO

Considering it's such a short word, no can be a hard one to say. Peer pressure, social pressure, pressure from adults, pressure to be perfect, pressure to be seen a certain way and pressure to be liked can all make that little word feel impossible to say out loud. But when it comes to your body boundaries, learning to say no – both in your head and out loud – is a vital piece of your toolkit. This counts both in terms of physical body boundaries, when someone wants to touch you, and also in terms of emotional body boundaries, when someone says something about your body. 'No' is a full sentence, and you never need to justify *why* you have said it, especially if it's about something that makes you feel uncomfortable in your body. (PS This includes when you don't want your mum to take a photo of you, or when you don't want to hug your nan at the next family Sunday lunch.)

RACE-BASED HAIR DISCRIMINATION

This is a form of racism where people are treated differently because their hair doesn't conform to white beauty standards. It might be that a Black pupil with an afro, for example, is expected to cut or straighten their hair, or that a student with bantu knots, locs or braids is told off because their hairstyle doesn't comply with their school's uniform policy. Students with natural or

protective hairstyles like these might also receive lots of comments, insults or unwanted attention simply because of the type of hair they have. This kind of discrimination doesn't only happen in schools. It affects adults in the workplace too.

Many activists and educators have been arguing for tighter protections for Black students under the law, to protect their right to wear their hair in natural styles and to express their identity and culture without fear of being told off, singled out or discriminated against. Knowing the emotional and cultural significance of Black hair is an important aspect of creating a world where all body boundaries are respected. It is never OK to ask to touch someone's hair, to make fun of their hair or to constantly make comments about it.

You're a big girl now!

DEALING WITH COMMENTS ABOUT YOUR APPEARANCE

It's not just negative comments about appearance that can be harmful. Even compliments made with the best of intentions can lead us to focus on how our bodies look instead of how they feel.

So here are five potential responses to someone commenting on your appearance. (FYI, you can use these for comments made both IRL and online.)

Haven't you grown!

- Yes, Aunty Wendy, I have grown. Did you know humans grow faster during puberty than at any other time in their lives, apart from when they are babies? Want to know some other amazing facts about the human body?

What a lovely figure you have . . .

- I know you mean that as a compliment, but I'd rather we talked about something else. I'm trying to have a healthy body image, and I've learned that focusing on how I look doesn't make me feel good.

Is that a new hairstyle?

- Yes, this is a new hairstyle. No, you can't touch it.

- Let me tell you about this amazing book/ film/TV show/[insert literally anything else that has nothing to do with your body here] that I've enjoyed.

Have you lost weight?

- Please don't talk about my body in that way, because it makes me uncomfortable.

If you notice that someone in your life persistently talks about your body, then you need to know that this isn't something you have to put up with. People aren't mind readers, so if they don't realize that their comments are making you uncomfortable they might continue to say them.

If the person is a family member who you don't see super regularly (like an aunt or uncle or someone else in your extended family), it might help to have a conversation with a trusted adult who can intervene on your behalf. If it's someone you're closer to, like a parent or your best friend, it might help to have a proper chat with them and explain why you don't want to hear these comments any more.

BODY-MYTH
ALERT: Building healthy body boundaries is selfish.

You might think that all this talk of saying no and learning how to build your own body boundaries means you'll become selfish. Actually, the opposite is true. There's some evidence to show that people with healthy boundaries are more likely to respect other people's boundaries, so developing good boundaries around how people treat your body will also help you to be more mindful of respecting the body boundaries of others.

Michelle Elman is a life coach, author, broadcaster and public speaker, and has written two books all about the importance of boundaries.

It is never OK to body shame, so if someone says something hurtful about your body, or makes an unwanted comment, put your boundaries down, stand up for your body and tell them to stop commenting on your body. Your body, your business!

Michelle Elman

RESPECTING OTHER PEOPLE'S BODY BOUNDARIES

So, we know that boundaries are not just about protecting ourselves – they're about protecting other people too. With that in mind, here are four steps to help you to respect and honour other people's body boundaries.

❶ DON'T MAKE ASSUMPTIONS

At the beginning of this chapter, we talked about how we are all different, and how the things one person likes, feels or experiences won't be the same as the next person. But sometimes it can be easy to forget this, and we make assumptions based on our own experiences. For example:

- someone who is tactile (which means they are quite touchy-feely) might expect everyone else to enjoy hugs as much as they do

- someone who has never felt pressure to look a certain way might think that comments about another's appearance are no big deal

- someone who has never been bullied based on the way they look or how their body functions may not notice when others are mistreated because of these things

Whatever your own experience may be, it's important to remember that not everyone is the same. But if you can try to see things from someone else's point of view, it will help you to respect their body boundaries.

❷ DON'T TAKE IT PERSONALLY

If you make a mistake and overstep someone else's body boundaries, and they say no, it might hurt your feelings. You might feel embarrassed or wonder what you did wrong, or you might feel angry or confused. The truth is, just as you have the right to decide how you want your body to be treated, other people have this right too. That includes your best friend, who you love to hug but doesn't love hugs themselves. And the new person at school who's got a cool haircut but would rather talk about something other than their hair. If someone doesn't receive a comment, compliment or hug in the way you expected they would, remember that this is just them setting a body boundary. Try to think about how you would like them to react if the roles were reversed.

❸ MOVE ON

When someone states a body boundary, as well as respecting their wishes, it's also important not to dwell on it in the moment. This just makes things awkward for everyone, including you! So don't try to persuade them otherwise, or have an argument about it, or make them justify why they don't want you to do something. Just say, 'OK cool', accept your own feelings and move on to something else that is way more interesting than having beef with someone about their body boundary.

❹ FEEL YOUR FEELINGS

All that being said, you are a human, not a robot, and your feelings are part of what makes you the brilliantly unique person you are. So, while it's important not to take someone else's body boundary as a sign of failure on your part and not to dwell on it, it's also important to recognize how it made you feel. This will help your brain to process the feeling and move on from it.

It might be that, at the time, you're unable to do this. But giving yourself some space to reflect on it later – maybe by writing in your journal or talking to a trusted adult – can help you to let out your feelings safely and not keep them bottled up.

BODY-MYTH ALERT: Avoiding appearance-based comments means you can never compliment someone's outfit.

You might think all this talk about boundaries means you should avoid ever talking about anything to do with the way someone presents themselves. But there is a big difference between complimenting someone's outfit because you love their style and complimenting someone's outfit because it makes them look thinner/ taller/more toned/[insert any other physical characteristic here].

Fashion and clothes can be a great way to express yourself, and this is something to be celebrated if it brings you joy. And recognizing when a friend has created an Insta-worthy outfit that you think looks totally cool isn't a bad thing. You're actually praising their creativity, individuality and unique spark when you do this. It has nothing to do with the body they were born with, which is probably not something you're interested in one bit anyway. (On another note, if you find clothes and fashion totally boring, that's cool too. The world would be a dull place if we were all into the same things!)

Finally, if you find yourself struggling for non-appearance-based conversation starters, here are five things that are way more interesting to chat about with someone than how they look.

WHAT THEY HAD FOR BREAKFAST.
(And do they know that the inventor of their breakfast cereal hated soft beds? Hi, Mr Kellogg!)

WHAT THEY'RE WATCHING ON NETFLIX.

WHETHER KOALAS ARE BETTER THAN PENGUINS.

CLEARLY, I'M THE COOLEST ONE HERE . . .

THE ULTIMATE SANDWICH FILLING.

LITERALLY ANYTHING ELSE IN THE WORLD.

THE BETTER WE ARE
AT BUILDING OUR OWN
HEALTHY BODY BOUNDARIES
AND RESPECTING THE BODY
BOUNDARIES OF OTHERS,
THE EASIER IT WILL
BE FOR EVERYBODY
TO FEEL GOOD.

Which leads us to the final part of this book . . .

CHAPTER 9

EVERY BODY

The way we think and feel about our bodies affects every aspect of our lives, but it also affects many aspects of our society. The judgements we make about our own bodies and about the bodies of others affect what we choose to spend our money on, how we spend our time and how we interact with those around us. This is as true for you as it is for the adults in your life – including the ones running your school, your sports clubs, your home and even your country. This is why body image is a **social-justice** issue.

WHAT IS SOCIAL JUSTICE?

Many of the things which affect our body image are things we need to change as a society, not as individuals. So, when it comes to finding solutions, we need to think bigger than just how we feel about our own bodies. This is where social justice comes in.

SOCIAL JUSTICE LOOKS AT HOW POWER AND PRIVILEGE ARE DISTRIBUTED AMONG PEOPLE IN SOCIETY, AND SEEKS TO MAKE THINGS MORE EQUAL FOR EVERYONE.

You might think this has nothing to do with you, because you're not an adult and you don't make the rules, but some of the most exciting social-justice movements and campaigns for social change have been led by people your age. As you've probably realized by now, adults don't know everything!

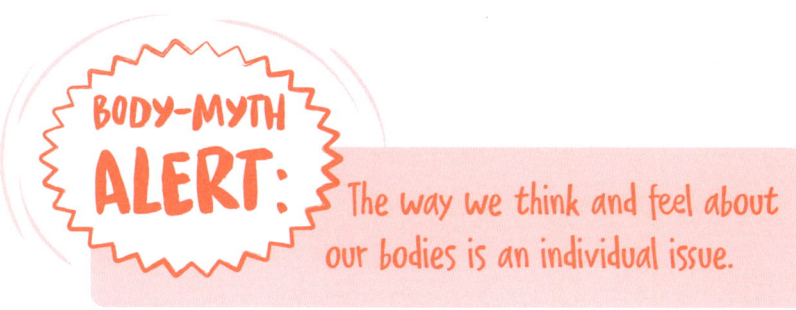

BODY-MYTH ALERT: The way we think and feel about our bodies is an individual issue.

Sometimes it might feel like having poor body image is something you need to solve by yourself, or as though you've failed somehow if you don't always love the body you're in. But remember, thinking about negative body image as a 'me' problem instead of a 'we' problem ignores all the societal factors which affect body image. While you can do things to help to protect your body image on an individual level (including many of the tips you've read in this book), it doesn't count for much if society is constantly giving you the message that your body is wrong, or not welcome, or not good enough exactly as it is.

These messages come in lots of different forms, from the way other people talk to you to how accessible the world is for your body. It might be hard to feel good in your body, for example, if you have a body that doesn't comfortably fit into the seats at the cinema, or if you use a wheelchair and the cinema doesn't have a lift or ramp to get inside. These are ways that society can make you feel left out, or like you need to change your body, when in fact the problem is society (and, in this case, the seats at the cinema or the lack of wheelchair ramp or lift), not your body.

The way we think and feel about our bodies is also affected by **social norms** – behaviours widely accepted as 'normal' – that come from diet culture. You might see these social norms in action when people talk about dieting, or comment on the way someone looks, or make the word 'fat' the punchline of a joke. All of these behaviours actively promote poor body image. Just imagine if we lived in a society where these types of actions were seen as weird or were called out. It would probably be a whole lot easier to feel good in our bodies.

BE THE CHANGE

Changing society – and, in this case, the parts of society that promote negative body image – is called **systemic change**.

SYSTEMIC CHANGE REQUIRES THE **COLLECTIVE ACTION** OF LOTS OF INDIVIDUAL PEOPLE WHO LIVE IN A SOCIETY, AND IT CAN START WITH **YOU!**

You might be thinking,

Blimey, this lady is full on. I'm not the Prime Minister. Surely the adults are the ones who need to sort this out.

And you wouldn't be wrong. But the thing is, we adults need your help. Some of the adults around you might not even be aware there's a problem, because they've never really thought about it before. (Like I said, adults don't know everything.)

YOU ARE A POWERFUL, INSPIRING PERSON.

Every single conversation you have with someone – either another person your age or one of the adults in your life – has an impact. Explaining to your best mate why you won't do that diet with them or telling your teacher when you hear about a body-shaming incident at school are brave ways you can create a ripple effect to make the world a happier place for *every*body.

Because of the way society is structured, there might be times when you don't feel safe to speak out. Perhaps you've been bullied yourself at school for your body, and the last thing you want to do is draw attention from the bullies again. You might feel it's safer to join in with body-shaming others, just to keep the heat off yourself. But this type of behaviour is what fuels inequality and body shame in the first place. It might not feel safe to challenge these conversations in the moment, but refusing to join in with them can be a powerful thing. And, later, you could raise it with a trusted adult who can help you to find a way to tackle this body-shaming culture in your school (or wherever it's happened).

USE YOUR PRIVILEGE TO MAKE A DIFFERENCE

If you've never been body-shamed or bullied for your body, then you may feel more confident about stepping in when you hear body-shaming conversations. This means you have a level of privilege that someone with a different experience from you might not have.

Perhaps your best mate has made a joke about the appearance of someone in your class, or you've overheard a group of kids making comments about someone's body in the playground. This is an opportunity to use your privilege and challenge the behaviour. Here are four suggested responses.

Amika George is an activist from the United Kingdom who started a campaign to get the British government to pledge free period products to all children in full-time education when she was just seventeen years old. In 2020, her Free Period campaign led to the government giving funding to all schools in England for free menstrual products for students.

I don't know why I thought I could be the one to do something, but something stirred in me. . . to look beyond the four walls of my comfortable bedroom, to put myself in the shoes of those girls who were too poor to have a period. Free Periods has taught me that activism really can change the world. That's why I believe everyone can, and should, be an activist.

Amika George

WHAT DOES BODY ACTIVISM LOOK LIKE?

Just as there's no one single way to have a body, there's no one single way to be a social-justice activist. The part that looks the same for every activist, though, is that they are all dedicated to making a positive change.

BODY FACT:
There are over three million people aged 10–14 in the UK.

WOAH.
THREE MILLION IS . . . A LOT.

Imagine what could happen if three million people did one small thing to make their communities more accepting places for *every*body? I'm no maths expert, but I bet it would be a lot easier for more people to be friends with their bodies.

Changing the world isn't easy or straightforward, though, which is why it's important to remember that even superheroes need a rest every now and again. The most

experienced activists and advocates will tell you that working towards social change can be a tiring business. It's a bit like cleaning your room and your little sister coming in and throwing a pile of dirty socks on the floor as soon as you've finished. It can feel like one step forwards, two (or ten) steps (or socks) back. That's why it's important to remember all the tips you've learned so far to take care of your mind and body, to rest, practise self-care and look after yourself.

OK, now, here's the really exciting bit:

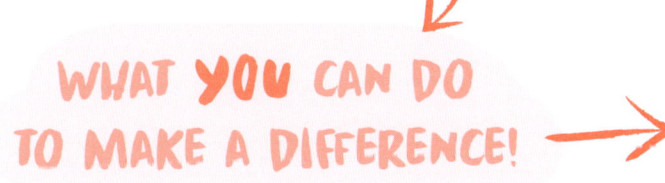

WHAT **YOU** CAN DO
TO MAKE A DIFFERENCE!

WRITE A LETTER

Never underestimate the power of a letter. If you see something that you think is going to make people feel bad about their body, like an advert for a diet brand on your school railings, write a letter! Depending on the thing you want to change (in this case, it would be getting the advert removed from your school railings), you will need to write to different people. Often the hardest bit is working out who to send your letter to, so if you're struggling you could ask a trusted adult to help you research this.

Perhaps you've noticed that your school doesn't include body-shaming in its anti-bullying policy, or you would like your local council to make your park more accessible for disabled children. All of these things start by writing letters to the people in charge of these areas and telling them why change needs to happen.

HOW TO WRITE A LETTER LIKE AN ACTIVIST

① **Find out who to write to** – it might be your headteacher, your councillor or your MP.

② **Write your address and the date** at the top of the letter.

③ If you know the name of the person you're writing to, **start the letter** with *Dear [insert their name here]*. If you don't know their name, write *Dear Sir or Madam* or *To Whom It May Concern*.

④ **Tell them who you are.** For example, *My name is [insert your name here] and I am an eleven-year-old pupil in [insert your teacher's name here]'s class*, or *My name is [insert your name here] and I am an eleven-year-old who lives in [insert your town/city here]*.

⑤ Explain why you are writing this letter.
For example, *I have noticed that body-shaming isn't clearly included in the school's anti-bullying policy, and I would like you to reconsider this.*

⑥ Explain why what you're asking for is so important. Don't be afraid to use your own personal, lived experience of the issue, if this is relevant. It can also help to include some facts and figures to back up your case. You could even use some of the body facts in this book!

⑦ End with a clear call to action, which is a request for exactly what you want to be done. For example, *Please include body-based bullying in the school anti-bullying policy and create displays celebrating body diversity in school.*

⑧ Be polite and respectful – you'll have a better chance of the person you're writing to considering your request if you speak to them in the way you would wish to be spoken to yourself. Also, there is a difference between being polite and being apologetic. Avoid saying things like *Sorry for sending this letter*, as this makes you sound as though you're unsure of what you're asking for. Instead, you could write something like, *Thank you for taking the time to read this letter and consider my request.*

9 If you know the name of the person you are writing to, **end your letter with *Yours sincerely***. If you don't know their name, end with *Yours faithfully*. Then write your name clearly at the bottom.

START AN ADVOCACY GROUP OR CLUB

The best change happens when you join forces with other people, so why not try to recruit new members to your mission? Perhaps you could start a Body Happy

Club or an **advocacy** group at school that is dedicated to creating a school environment where *every*body is given the chance to be friends with their body. It would only take a few members to make an action plan and start turning your ideas into reality. Club projects could include:

- asking your teachers to help you to create a body-positive display in the school hall

- writing an article about body positivity for the school newsletter

- encouraging your school to introduce a full week of activities dedicated to lovely things like joyful movement, mindfulness, self-care and body image advocacy

DON'T BE AFRAID TO DREAM BIG!

START A BODY-POSITIVE BOOK-SHARING CIRCLE

If you've read this far, I'm guessing that you're a book fan like me. (Book fans unite!) Books can be a brilliant window on to the world, and a way to learn about new things. This is true for all subjects, including body image. Helping to introduce books about body image to new readers is an act of advocacy in itself. The more people who read these books, the more that people in general will be aware of the issue and their role in creating change.

You can make this happen by, for example, emailing your school or local library and asking them to stock more body positive books (you can find some ideas at the back of this book). You could also start a sharing circle with your friends, where you swap titles on this subject then have a chat about them once you've all finished reading. Not everyone is a book lover, which is totally cool – but, for those who are, connecting over a shared interest and passion can be a brilliant thing.

START A COMPLIMENTS CHAIN

Random acts of kindness are the absolute best. They make the giver feel good, and the receiver gets an instant burst of happiness. You could start a compliments chain at your school or among your group of friends to help remind people that they are so much more than their body. Everyone can take a compliment whenever they're in need of a pep-talk!

There are lots of ways to do this. For instance, you could write non-appearance-based compliments on slips of paper then give them out to your friends.

Another idea is to keep the compliments in a jar, then share them with your family at home or even with your class at school. There's just one rule: if you take a compliment, you need to replace it with your own to keep the jar full!

BECOMING THE ACTIVIST YOU ARE MEANT TO BE

There is no single way to be a body activist. And, importantly, it isn't just another thing to add to your to-do list. I know you're busy, so the last thing you need is *more* homework. These are just some ideas to get you started, but maybe you've got some ideas of your own?

You don't need to do any of these things to be an activist, though.

SIMPLY HAVING CONVERSATIONS WITH THE PEOPLE IN YOUR LIFE AND NOT ENGAGING IN BODY TALK ARE TWO POWERFUL ACTIONS THAT DON'T COST A THING AND CAN MAKE A HUGE DIFFERENCE.

AND FINALLY . . .

Now it's time to say goodbye, which is not something I'm any good at. I often cry at goodbyes, so as you're reading this, imagine me sitting at my desk typing with tears and snot dripping on to my keyboard. Before we say the final, final goodbye, let's do a little recap. (If this were a YouTube video, there'd be some sentimental-yet-inspirational music playing, so maybe you could imagine that too.)

- We started this book thinking about YOUR body and all the amazing things it lets you do.

- We've learned to celebrate ALL bodies and the wonderful diversity of humankind.

- We've talked about the pressure to have a GOOD body, and where harmful appearance standards come from.

- We've unpicked some of the RULES for bodies, and how to separate good ones from bad ones.

- We've discovered how to RESPECT our bodies (and others' bodies too), and appreciate them for the miracle they are.

- We've learned to spot FILTERED bodies, and understand how the internet can distort our body image.

- And we've practised saying NOT YOUR BODY and using our voices to stand up for EVERY BODY.

I hope that everything you've learned in this book will help you on your way to feeling at home in your body, to being kind to both your body and others' bodies, and to feeling empowered to create change (however small) so that EVERYBODY knows that their body is good enough exactly as it is.

GLOSSARY

A

Ableism: Discrimination and social prejudice against disabled people.

Accessibility / accessible: Equal access for disabled people to an environment, product or service. For example, a building could be made more accessible by fitting a wheelchair ramp or wheelchair lift to the entrance so that anyone unable to use the stairs can still access the building.

Activist: A person who campaigns and takes direct action to bring about change in society.

Adultification: A type of discrimination that sees some children thought of (and treated) as more grown-up than they actually are. This can mean they are given more responsibility, or seen as less innocent, than other kids the same age. Adultification bias is the held view or prejudice that leads to this discrimination.

Advocacy: Supporting a cause and standing up for something.

Anti-fat bias: Prejudiced beliefs and assumptions made about fat people. (Reminder: in this book, we use the word 'fat' as a neutral descriptor. Fat is not a bad word.)

Appearance pressure: External pressure which makes us feel we need to look a certain way.

Beauty standards: A set of standards that define what we think of as attractive. Beauty standards will change depending on the culture, period and what is in fashion at any one time.

Body acceptance: Accepting your body as it is, even if you don't love every aspect of it.

Body appreciation: Appreciating what your body does for you and how it allows you to live your life.

Body diversity: The ways that our bodies are all different.

Body ideals: The body type promoted by society as being the best. Body ideals can change, depending on what is in fashion at the time.

Body neutrality: The ability to accept and respect your body, however it looks or functions, and to know that your body is not the most important thing about you.

Body positivity movement: A social movement focused on the liberation of marginalised bodies that are often discriminated against by society, and on the celebration and acceptance of all bodies.

Body privilege: The ways we benefit from advantages granted to us purely based on the way we look or the way our bodies function.

Colourism: A type of discrimination based on skin colour, where people with darker skin are treated differently and experience less privilege and more disadvantages than people with lighter skin.

Confirmation bias: The tendency to process new information in a way that confirms or backs up our existing beliefs.

Diet culture: A system of beliefs equating thinness with health, morality, beauty and other perceived positive traits.

Disability: Any physical or mental difference that makes it more difficult for someone to participate in activities as easily as someone whose body or brain does not work in the same way.

DNA: Genetic information inside the body's cells that makes us who we are. It's a self-replicating material that exists in most living things and carries the blueprint or 'code' for that particular organism (or person!).

Embodiment: The lived experience of being in a body and focusing on how it feels instead of how it looks.

Equality: Equal treatment, access, opportunities and resources for all people.

Executive functions: The mental processes that help us plan, focus our attention, do more than one thing at once, remember things, and have control over our emotions, behaviours and impulses.

Gender binary: The idea that there are only two genders.

Gender identity: The personal sense someone has of their own gender.

Gender norms: Unwritten rules for behaving a certain way based on your gender.

Gender stereotypes: Beliefs and assumptions that assign certain characteristics to a person based on their gender.

Genes: The basic unit of heredity that exists inside our cells and determines the traits passed down from biological parent to child.

Healthism: The belief that health is all down to the individual and their personal lifestyle choices. This belief system doesn't acknowledge the many things that have an affect on a person's health but are beyond their individual control.

Interoception: The process of tuning in to your body, and how you perceive the senses and feelings within it.

Media literacy: The ability to think critically and analytically about the media we are consuming in order to evaluate its accuracy, intent and impact.

Mental health: Our emotional, psychological and social wellbeing.

Neurodiversity: Diversity (the range of differences) in the ways our brains all function, and the ways this might make us behave and experience the world.

Neurodivergent: A way of describing people whose brains work in a different way from what is considered more common in people of their age and in their culture.

Neurotypical: A way of describing people whose brains work in a similar way to what is considered more common to other people their age and in their culture.

Positive affirmation: A positive phrase or statement that can be used to challenge negative or unhelpful thoughts.

Race science: A genre of pretend science based on the made-up belief that humans can be divided into biologically distinct categories based on skin colour and other features, and that this can be used to justify racism.

Systemic change: Change that happens across all parts of a system (instead of just one part) to solve social problems and create lasting change. Systemic change deals with the root cause of a problem, rather than just the symptoms of it.

Social determinants of health: The economic and social conditions which affect (or determine) our health. This includes where we live, our access to education and healthcare, how much money we have, and the support and connection we have with our communities.

Social justice: Equal rights, opportunities and treatment for all people.

Social model of disability: A way of looking at disability that says people are disabled by the barriers of society rather than their differences. These barriers might be physical (such as stairs and a lack of wheelchair ramps) or it might be other people's attitudes to disability.

Social norms: The unwritten or informal rules which are thought of as acceptable and normal in society.

Societal issue: A problem which affects many people within a society.

Weight stigma: The discrimination and stereotyping of fat people.

SOURCES

Multiple sources were consulted in the writing of this book – here is a selection of some of the key books and articles that were used. Note that in some cases, the sources below use different language and terminology to that used in this book.

CHAPTER 1: MY BODY

p.11: Nadia Craddock quoted in Forbes, Molly, *Body Happy Kids*. (London: Vermilion, 2021)

p.13: Sam Smith quoted in 'Sam Smith x Jameela Jamil on body image and self acceptance | I Weigh Interviews', www.youtube.com, 12 June 2020

p.20: Rudd Center for Food Policy and Obesity, www.uconnruddcenter.org

CHAPTER 2: ALL BODIES

p.35: Will, Manuel, Stock, Jay T., 'Spatial and temporal variation of body size among early Homo', *Journal of Human Evolution*, Volume 82, May 2015, pages 15–33

p.35: 'Earliest humans had diverse range of body types, just as we do today', www.cam.ac.uk, 27 Mar 2015

p.36–7: 'climatic-adaptation', www.britannica.com

p.36–7: Dorey, Fran, 'How have we changed since our species first appeared?', australian.museum, 8 Feb 2021

p.40: Trina Nicole quoted in March, Bridget, 'Body inclusivity champion Trina Nicole on why it's important to unapologetically take up space', *Harper's Bazaar*, www.harpersbazaar.com, 23 Feb 2022

p.44: Girma, Haben, *Haben: The Deafblind Woman Who Conquered Harvard Law.* (New York: NY: Twelve Books, 2019)

CHAPTER 3: GOOD BODY

p.55–58: Strings, Sabrina, *Fearing the Black Body: The Racial Origins of Fat Phobia.* (New York, NY: NYU Press, 2019)

p.56–7: 'Sarah Baartman', kids.britannica.com

p.68: Johnnie Tillmon quote in Tillmon, Johnnie, 'Welfare is a Women's Issue', *MS Magazine*, www.msmagazine.com, Spring 1972

p.70: Judy Freespirit quoted in Bracha Fishman, Sarah Golda, 'Life in the Fat Underground', *Radiance Magazine Online*, www.radiancemagazine.com, Winter 1998

CHAPTER 4: RULES FOR BODIES

p.85: Yasmin Finney quoted in O'Malley, Katie, 'Yasmin Finney On 'Heartstopper', Trans Representation And Authenticity', *Elle*, www.elle.com, 9 May 2022

p.97–98: 'Business of Beauty: A Resource Guide', guides. loc.gov/business-of-beauty

p.98: Berg, Achim, Hudson, Sara, Klitsch Weaver, Kristi, Lesko Pacchia, Megan and Amed, Imran, 'The beauty market in 2023: A special State of Fashion report', www.mckinsey.com /industries/retail/our-insights/ the-beauty-market-in-2023-a-special-state-of-fashion-report, 23 May 2022

CHAPTER 5: RESPECTED BODY

p.110: Goudie, Shona, 'New data show 4 million children in households affected by food insecurity', www.foodfoundation.org.uk/publication/new-data-show-4-million-children-households-affected-food-insecurity, 18 Oct 2022

p.116: 'Body image report – Executive Summary', mentalhealth.org.uk/explore-mental-health/articles/ body-image-report-executive-summary

p.116: Lally, P., van Jaarsveld, C.H.M., Potts, H.W.W. and Wardle, J., 'How are habits formed: Modelling habit formation in the real world', *European Journal of Social Psychology,* Volume 40, Oct 2010, pages 998–1009

p.136: Ahmad A., Little M, Piernas C., et al., 'Trends in weight loss attempts among children in England', *Archives of Disease in Childhood,* Oct 2022, Volume 107, pages 896–901

p.138: Memon A. N., Gowda A. S., Rallabhandi B., et al., 'Have Our Attempts to Curb Obesity Done More Harm Than Good?', *Cureus,* Volume 12:9, 6 Sept 2020

p.138: 'Statistics', Center of Excellence for Eating Disorders, www.med.unc.edu/psych/eatingdisorders/learn-more/about-eating-disorders/statistics/

p.143: Cody Miller quoted in Lohn, John, 'Champion's Mojo Podcast: A Chat With Breaststroke Star Cody Miller', www.swimmingworldmagazine.com/news/champions-mojo-podcast-a-chat-with-breaststroke-star-cody-miller/

p.142–143: Duncan, L.R., Hall, C.R., Wilson, P.M. et al., 'Exercise motivation: a cross-sectional analysis examining its relationships with frequency, intensity, and duration of exercise', *International Journal of Behavioral Nutrition and Physical Activity*, Volume 7:7, 26 Jan 2010

p.150–151: Calum Neill, Janelle Gerard & Katherine D. Arbuthnott, 'Nature contact and mood benefits: contact duration and mood type', The Journal of Positive Psychology, Volume 14:6, 2019, pages 756–767

p.152–153: Smith, Becca, 'Kindness: Paying It Forward to Improve Your Well-Being', www.ie.edu/center-for-health-and-well-being /blog/benefits-of-kindness-and-paying-it-forward, 28 April 2023

CHAPTER 6: MIRACLE BODY

p.159: Breehl, L., Caban, O., 'Physiology, Puberty', StatPearls Publishing LLC, 2023

p.163: Davis, Jahnine, 'Adultification bias within child protection and safeguarding', HM Inspectorate of Probation, Academic Insights June 2022

p.165: 'Early or delayed puberty', www.nhs.uk/conditions/early-or-delayed-puberty/

p.169: Yesudian P., 'Human hair – an evolutionary relic?', *International Journal of Trichology*. Volume 3:2, July 2011

p.169–170: Alex, Bridget, 'Why Humans Lost Their Hair and Became Naked and Sweaty', www.discovermagazine.com/planet-earth/why-humans-lost-their-hair-and-became-naked-and-sweaty, 17 Jan 2019

p.172–173: Cerini, Marianna, 'Why women feel pressured to shave', edition.cnn.com/style/article/why-women-feel-pressured-to-shave/, 3 March 2020

p.174–175: Kaur, Harnaam, 'Empowerment through confidence', TEDxWarwick, www.ted.com/talks harnaam_kaur_empowerment_through_confidence, March 2018

p.186: 'In conversation with skin positivity influencer Constanza Concha', ohmymag.co.uk, 8 Feb 2022

p.187–189: 'Starting your periods', www.nhs.uk/conditions/periods/

p.187: Rohatgi, A., Dash, S., 'Period poverty and mental health of menstruators during COVID-19 *pandemic: Lessons and implications for the future*', *Frontiers in Global Women's Health*, Volume 4, 2023

p.189: 'Periods: Overview', www.nhs.uk/conditions/
periods/starting-periods/

p.193: Kenny Ethan Jones quoted in Ethan Jones, Kenny,
'Mental health matters with Kenny Ethan Jones',
www.happiful.com /mental-health-matters-with-kenny-
ethan-jones, 30 April 2020

p.194: Pliny, *The Natural History*. John Bostock M.D., F.R.S.
H.T. Riley, Esq., B.A. (London: Taylor and Francis, 1855)

p.194: Kovac, Milan, 'Maya Female Taboo: Menstruation
and Pregnancy in Lacandon Daily Life', Contributions in
New World Archaeology, 2017

CHAPTER 7: FILTERED BODY

p.213: Meeker, Mary, 'Internet Trends 2016—Code
Conference,' Kleiner Perkins Caufield & Byers,
cacm.acm.org/news/203062-internet-trends-2016-code-
conference/fulltext, June 2016

p.213: Morrison, Sean, 'Average person takes more than
450 selfies every year, study finds', www.standard.co.uk,
19 Dec 2019

p.221: Kim Chi quoted in Moon, Rebecca, 'Drag queen
Kim Chi talks Korean pride and her 'full circle' moment

with her queer POC makeup line', www.nextshark.com, 1 April 2022

p.226: Abrams, Zara, 'How can we minimize Instagram's harmful effects?', *Monitor on Psychology: American Psychological Association*, Volume 53: 2, 2 Dec 2021

p.226: Cohen, R., Fardouly, J., Newton-John, T., & Slater, A., '#BoPo on Instagram: An experimental investigation of the effects of viewing body positive content on young women's mood and body image', *New Media & Society*, Volume 21:7, 2019, pages 1546–1564

p.226: Brown, Z., Tiggemann, M., 'Attractive celebrity and peer images on Instagram: Effect on women's mood and body image', *Body Image*, Volume 19, Dec 2019, pages 37–43

CHAPTER 8: NOT YOUR BODY

p.240: 'Why do you itch and should you scratch?', *The Curious Cases of Rutherford and Fry*, www.bbc.co.uk

p.241: Cascio, C.J., Moana-Filho, E.J., Guest, S., Nebel, M.B., Weisner, J., Baranek, G.T., Essick, G.K., 'Perceptual and neural response to affective tactile texture stimulation in adults with autism spectrum disorders',

Autism Research, Volume 5:4, Aug 2012, pages 231–44

p.244: 'Study finds that genes play a role in empathy', www.cam.ac.uk, 12 March 2018

p.252: Lebow, Hilary I., 'How to Be Assertive Without Being Aggressive', www.psychcentral.com, 24 Aug 2022

p.253: Quote from Michelle Elman provided bespoke for this book.

CHAPTER 9: EVERY BODY

p.269: George, Amika, 'How I helped convince the U.K. to provide free period products in schools', www.washingtonpost.com, 25 May 2022

p.270: 'Population of England in 2021, by age group', www.statista.com, 26 Sept 2023

FURTHER SUPPORT AND READING

In this book we've explored body image and the problems it can sometimes cause, which will affect some people more than others. If you or anyone you know are struggling with any of the issues raised in this book, then it's important to speak to a trusted adult. They can help you to seek professional support if you need it, and your doctor is always a good place to start. Here is a list of resources and organizations that may be useful for you and your grown-ups.

MENTAL HEALTH SUPPORT

YoungMinds – mental health charity for children and young people www.youngminds.org.uk

Place2Be – children and young people's mental health charity www.place2be.org.uk

The Mix – mental health support for under 25s www.themix.org.uk

WORKSHOPS FOR SCHOOLS AND RESOURCES FOR KIDS

Body Happy Organisation – the social enterprise that I run. Tell your grown-ups to look us up! www.bodyhappyorg.com

OTHER BOOKS THAT TACKLE BODY IMAGE ISSUES

Karma Khullar's Mustache by Kristi Wientge

Jemima Small Versus the Universe by Tamsin Winter

Starfish by Lisa Fipps

Fat Chance Charlie Vega by Crystal Maldonado

EVERY BODY

ACKNOWLEDGEMENTS

Writing a book is a bit like doing a three-year extended homework project, except it's a project that loads of people help you with. This includes the people who tentatively listen to your idea before you've even committed it to paper (in my case this is my husband Simon, who is unendingly supportive of me and my work, even when I am going on and on and on . . . and on about it). The people who help you shape the idea before sending it out to publishers to see if anyone else thinks it's a good idea too (thanks here go to the incredible Lauren, Justine and Julie at Bell Lomax Moreton). The people who believe in the idea and polish it into something even more special (Meg and Phoebe at Puffin, I'm looking at you). And the people who turn that idea into a reality (it's Meg and Phoebe again, and all the wonderful team at Puffin who absolutely understood the assignment and breathed such vibrant life into this book it literally bursts off the page).

Extra special thanks go to Mollie Cronin who somehow stepped inside my head and created the most beautiful artwork to make the words sing. This book would just be a boring collection of letters without Mollie's incredible talent. The fact we share a name is the icing on the cake.

Before I handed my extra-big homework project – oops. I mean book – in, I had a brilliantly clever bunch of people read it (or parts of it) for me. Not just the people who check for important stuff like grammar and spellings (and bad fart jokes) at Puffin, but also people who looked over the contents of the book and decided if it was good enough and helpful enough to be something they would recommend. *Every Body* had an amazing team of checkers, which includes a crew of pilot readers aged 9–13. Thank you to Grace Jelley, Hazel and Elwood Scott and Freya and Effie Weaver. You are all very much appreciated. Plus, the super brainy adults: Dr Chantell Douglas who is a child psychologist, Aya Wingate who is a children's eating disorder dietitian, Victoria Henry who is a Year 6 teacher and PSHE leader, and Dr Asher Larmie who is a GP and weight stigma expert. Thank you for sharing your time, expertise and valuable thoughts to make this book what it is.

Finally, everyone who has ever done a big homework project knows you need cheerleaders to keep you going with words of encouragement, snacks and occasionally a shoulder to cry on when it all feels a bit much. For me, this was my family and friends. You know who you are. I am very lucky to have such wonderful people in my life, even when I'm being very annoying, crying down the phone, leaving podcast length voice-notes, locking myself away for days on end ignoring everyone, and being grumpier than Squidward from *SpongeBob SquarePants*. Thank you for putting up with me, I love you all very much.

Every Body would not exist without the trailblazers who have lit the way before it. Thank you to everyone who is working to make the world a more accepting place for *all* bodies, including every single person quoted in this book.

And, now that the homework is complete and it's time to hand it in, I want to thank YOU. Thank you, lovely reader, for being my teacher, for reading this book and considering its message. I hope you've found it helpful. It's been a privilege to write for you. I'm sorry there weren't enough fart jokes, I'll do better next time.

MF x

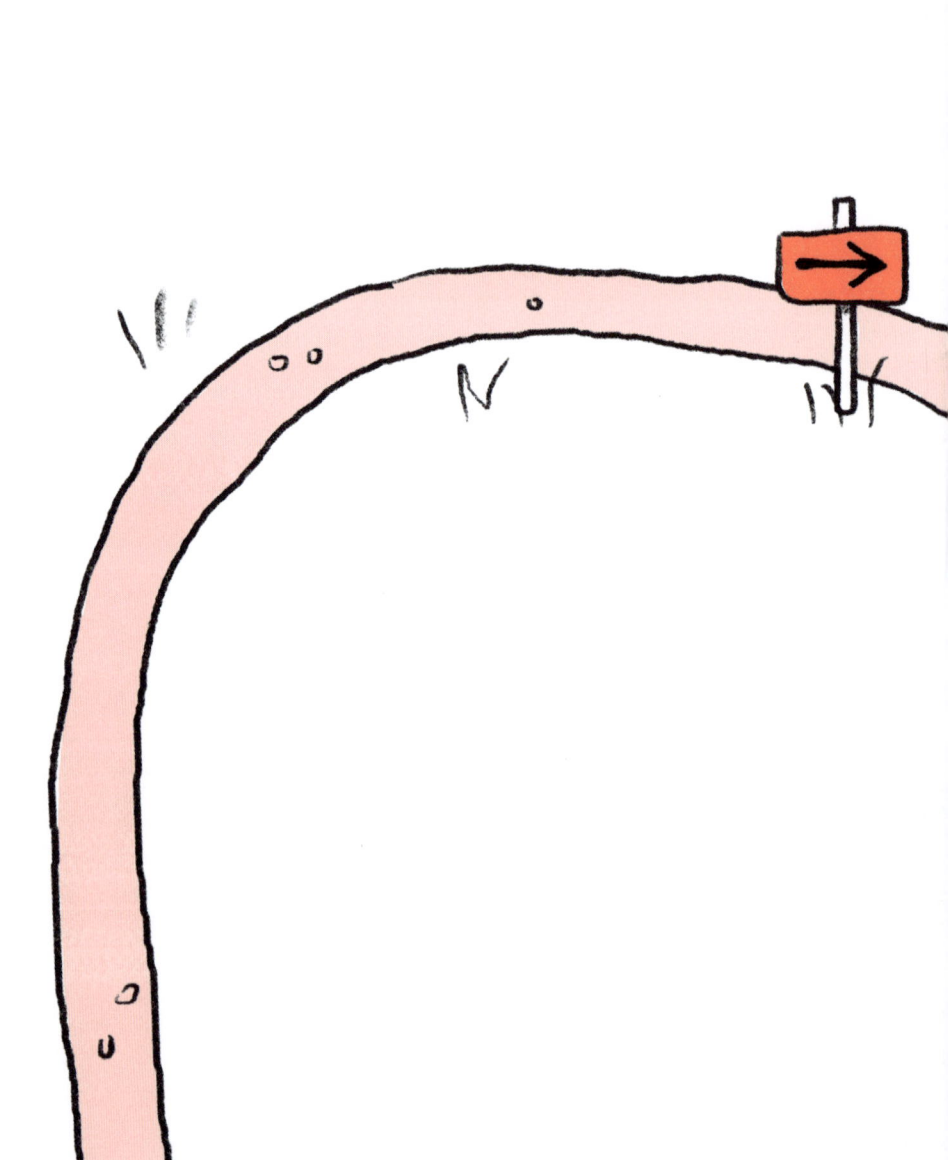

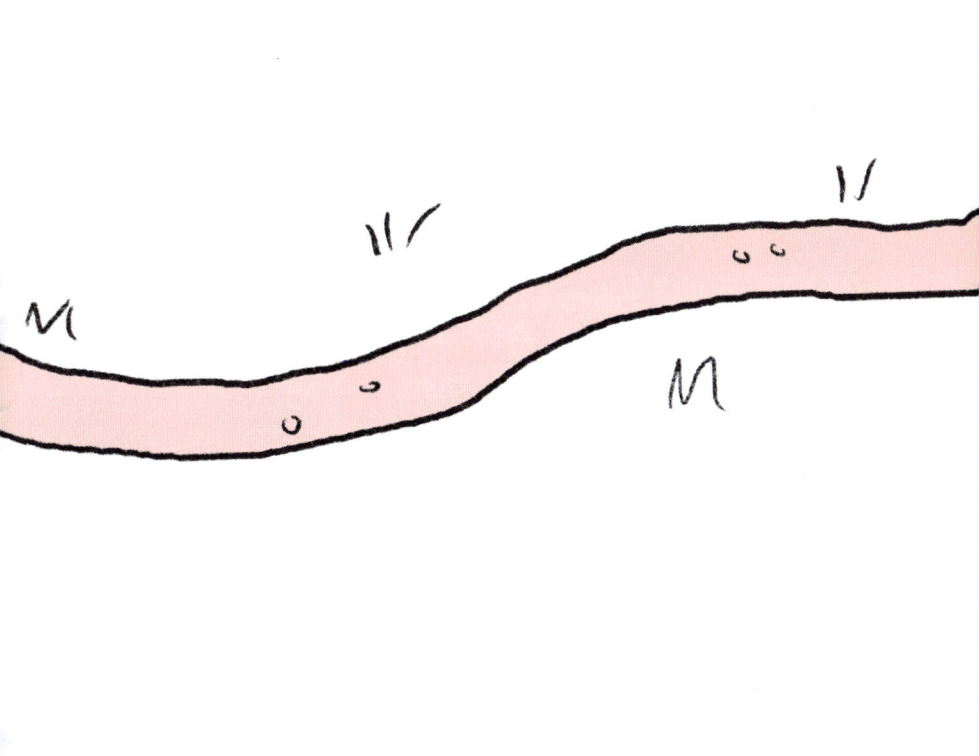

THANK YOU, EVERY BODY.